EVOLVE

STUDENT'S BOOK

with Digital Pack

Leslie Anne Hendra, Mark Ibbotson,
and Kathryn O'Dell

1A

 CAMBRIDGE
UNIVERSITY PRESS

Shaftesbury Road, Cambridge CB2 8EA, United Kingdom

One Liberty Plaza, 20th Floor, New York, NY 10006, USA

477 Williamstown Road, Port Melbourne, VIC 3207, Australia

314–321, 3rd Floor, Plot 3, Splendor Forum, Jasola District Centre, New Delhi – 110025, India

103 Penang Road, #05-06/07, Visioncrest Commercial, Singapore 238467

Cambridge University Press & Assessment is a department of the University of Cambridge.

We share the University's mission to contribute to society through the pursuit of education, learning and research at the highest international levels of excellence.

www.cambridge.org
Information on this title: www.cambridge.org/9781009231770

First published with Digital Pack 2022

20 19 18 17 16 15 14 13

Printed in Poland by Opolgraf

A catalogue record for this publication is available from the British Library

ISBN 978-1-009-23167-1 Student's Book with eBook
ISBN 978-1-009-23176-3 Student's Book with Digital Pack
ISBN 978-1-009-23177-0 Student's Book with Digital Pack A
ISBN 978-1-009-23178-7 Student's Book with Digital Pack B
ISBN 978-1-108-40894-3 Workbook with Audio
ISBN 978-1-108-40859-2 Workbook with Audio A
ISBN 978-1-108-41191-2 Workbook with Audio B
ISBN 978-1-108-40512-6 Teacher's Edition with Test Generator
ISBN 978-1-108-41062-5 Presentation Plus
ISBN 978-1-108-41201-8 Class Audio CDs
ISBN 978-1-108-40791-5 Video Resource Book with DVD
ISBN 978-1-009-23149-7 Full Contact with Digital Pack

Additional resources for this publication at www.cambridge.org/evolve

ACKNOWLEDGMENTS

The *Evolve* publishers would like to thank the following individuals and institutions who have contributed their time and insights into the development of the course:

Ivanova Monteros A., **Universidad Tecnológica Equinoccial (UTE)**, Ecuador; Monica Frenzel, **Universidad Andrés Bello**, Chile; Antonio Machuca Montalvo, **Organización The Institute TITUELS**, Veracruz, Mexico; Daniel Martin, **CELLEP**, Brazil; Roberta Freitas, **IBEU**, Brazil; Verónica Nolivos Arellano, Language Coordinator, Quito, Ecuador; Daniel Lowe, **Lowe English Services**, Panama; Maria Araceli Hernández Tovar, **Instituto Tecnológico Superior de San Luis Potosí**, Capital, Mexico; Lenise Butler, **Laureate**, Mexico; Gloria González Meza, **Instituto Politecnico Nacional, ESCA (University)**, Mexico; Miguel Ángel López, **Universidad Europea de Madrid**, Spain; Diego Ribeiro Santos, **Universidade Anhembi Morumbi**, São Paulo, Brazil; Esther Carolina Euceda Garcia, **UNITEC (Universidad Tecnologica Centroamericana)**, Honduras.

To our student cast, who have contributed their ideas and their time, and who appear throughout this book:

Anderson Batista, Brazil; Carolina Nascimento Negrão, Brazil; Felipe Martinez Lopez, Mexico; Jee-Hyo Moon, South Korea ; Jinny Lara, Honduras; Josue Lozano, Honduras; Julieth C. Moreno Delgado, Colombia; Larissa Castro, Honduras.

And special thanks to Katy Simpson, teacher and writer at *myenglishvoice.com*; and Raquel Ribeiro dos Santos, EFL teacher, EdTech researcher, blogger, and lecturer.

Authors' Acknowledgments:

The authors would like to extend their warmest thanks to all of the team at Cambridge University Press who were involved in creating this course. In particular, they would like to thank Ruby Davies and Robert Williams for their kindness, enthusiasm, and encouragement throughout the writing of the A1 level. They would also like to express their appreciation to Caroline Thiriau, whose understanding and support have been of great value. And they would like to thank Katie La Storia for her dedication and enthusiasm throughout the project.

Kathryn O'Dell would like to thank her parents (and grandparents) for passing down a love for words and stories. She also thanks her husband, Kevin Hurdman, for his loving support.

Leslie Anne Hendra would like to thank Michael Stuart Clark, her *sine qua non*, for his support and encouragement during this and other projects.

Mark Ibbotson would like to thank Aimy and Tom for their patience and understanding as family life was bent and squeezed around the project, and – especially – Nathalie, whose energy and creative solutions made it all possible.

The authors and publishers acknowledge the following sources of copyright material and are grateful for the permissions granted. While every effort has been made, it has not always been possible to identify the sources of all the material used, or to trace all copyright holders. If any omissions are brought to our notice, we will be happy to include the appropriate acknowledgements on reprinting and in the next update to the digital edition, as applicable.

Photo:

Key: B = Below, BG = Background, BL = Below Left, BR = Below Right, C = Centre, CL = Centre Left, CR = Centre Right, L = Left, R = Right, TC = Top Centre, TL = Top Left, TR = Top Right.

All images are sourced from Getty Images.

p. xvi (listen): Tara Moore/DigitalVision; p. xvi (say): Tara Moore/The Image Bank; p. xvi (write): Kohei Hara/DigitalVision; p. xvi (watch): Felbert+Eickenberg/Stock4B; p. xvi (students): Klaus Vedfelt/DigitalVision; p. 1, p. 2 (Gabi), p. 8 (CR), p. 14 (L), p. 36 (email): Hero Images; p. 2 (Karina): oscarhdez/iStock/Getty Images Plus; p. 2 (Antonio): Vladimir Godnik; p. 2 (Max): DMEPhotography/iStock/Getty Images Plus; p. 2 (map): Colormos/The Image Bank; p. 2 (network): OktalStudio/DigitalVision Vectors; p. 2 (globe): Image by Catherine MacBride/Moment; p. 4: Tara Moore/Taxi; p. 4, p. 6, p. 22 (living room), p. 24 (lamp), p. 52 (CR), p. xvi (read): Westend61; p. 7: ATGImages/iStock Editorial/Getty Images Plus; p. 8 (1.1a): .shock/iStock/Getty Images Plus; p. 8 (1.1b): Carl Olsson/Folio Images; p. 8 (1.1c): Phil Boorman/Cultura; p. 8 (1.1d), p. 54 (college), p. 62 (photo h): Caiaimage/Sam Edwards; p. 8 (1.1e): Mark Edward Atkinson/Blend Images; p. 8 (1.1f): Thomas Northcut/DigitalVision; p. 8 (1.1g), p. 36 (man), p. 37, p. 49 (CR): Sam Edwards/Caiaimage; p. 8 (1.1h): Glow Images, Inc/Glow; p. 8 (BR): Alistair Berg/DigitalVision; p. 9 (L): ajr_images/iStock/Getty Images Plus; p. 9 (R): Ivan Evgenyev/Blend Images; pp. 10, 20, 30, 42, 52, 62: Tom Merton/Caiaimage; p. 10 (photo a): Georges De Keerle/Hulton Archive; p. 10 (photo b): Monica Schipper/FilmMagic; p. 10 (photo c): DEA/D.

DAGLI ORTI/De Agostini; p. 10 (photo d): Scott Gries/Getty Images Entertainment; p. 10 (photo e, i): Bettmann; p. 10 (photo f): Sgranitz/WireImage; p. 10 (photo g): Christopher Furlong/Getty Images News; p. 10 (photo h): Dan Kitwood/Getty Images Entertainment; p. 10 (photo j): ALFREDO ESTRELLA/AFP; p. 11: Thomas Barwick/Stone; p. 13: Paco Navarro/Blend Images; p. 14 (couple), p. 20: Ronnie Kaufman/Larry Hirshowitz/Blend Images; p. 14 (Erika): Tony Anderson/DigitalVision; p. 14 (boy): Flashpop/Stone; p. 14 (woman): aldomurillo/E+; p. 16: Alyson Aliano/Image Source; p. 17: Richard Jung/Photodisc; p. 18: powerofforever/E+; p. 19: Steve Prezant/Image Source; p. 21, p. 30 (chair): Johner Images; p. 22 (bedroom): svetikd/E+; p. 22 (bathroom): JohnnyGreig/E+; p. 24 (bed): Diane Auckland/ArcaidImages; p. 24 (chair): Daniel Grill; p. 24 (table): Steve Gorton/Dorling Kindersley; p. 24 (desk): pbombaert/Moment; p. 24 (bookcase): Andreas von Einsiedel/Corbis Documentary; p. 24 (couch): Fotosearch; p. 24 (shower): RollingEarth/E+; p. 24 (refrigerator): Karen Moskowitz/The Image Bank; p. 24 (TV): Tetra Images; p. 24 (sink): Mark Griffin/EyeEm; p. 24 (rug): Art-Y/E+; p. 25: Hinterhaus Productions/Taxi; p. 26 (coffee): Dobroslav Hadzhiev/iStock/Getty Images Plus; p. 26 (tea): a-poselenov/iStock/Getty Images Plus; p. 26 (sugar): Maximilian Stock Ltd./Photographer's Choice; p. 26 (milk): YelenaYemchuk/iStock/Getty Images Plus; p. 26 (cookie): SvetlanaKoryakova/iStock/Getty Images Plus; p. 27: Shestock/Blend Images; p. 28 (TL): Hinterhaus Productions/DigitalVision; p. 29 (TR): Lilly Bloom/Cultura; p. 30 (TL): PeopleImages/DigitalVision; p. 30 (sofa): jakkapan21/iStock/Getty Images Plus; p. 30 (bookcase): Hany Rizk/EyeEm; p. 30 (couch): Nicholas Eveleigh/Photodisc; p. 30 (bed): Artem Perevozchikov/iStock/Getty Images Plus; p. 30 (desk): tifonimages/iStock/Getty Images Plus; p. 30 (chair): SKrow/iStock/Getty Images Plus; p. 30 (refrigerator): Customdesigner/iStock/Getty Images Plus; p. 30 (TV1): Dovapi/iStock/Getty Images Plus; p.30 (TV2): Jorg Greuel/Photographer's Choice RF; p. 30 (dining): s-cphoto/E+; p. 30 (frame): Matthias Clamer/Stone; p.30 (rug): Chaloner Woods/Hulton Archive; p. 30 (lamp): xxmmxx/E+; p. 30 (plant), p. 61 (BG): Dorling Kindersley; p. 33: VCG/Getty Images News; p. 34 (tablet): daboost/iStock/Getty Images Plus; p. 34 (earphone): Dave King/Dorling Kindersleyl; p. 34 (phone): Lonely_/iStock/Getty Images Plus; p. 34 (laptop): scanrail/iStock/Getty Images Plus; p. 34 (smartwatch): Nerthuz/iStock/Getty Images Plus; p. 35: Images By Tang Ming Tung/DigitalVision; p. 36 (cellphone): hocus-focus/iStock/Getty Images Plus; p. 36 (chat): David Malan/The Image Bank; p. 36 (tab, text): ymgerman/iStock Editorial/Getty Images Plus; p. 36 (game): Keith Bell/Hemera/Getty Images Plus; p. 36 (phone): Bloomberg; p. 36 (symbol): jaroszpilewski/iStock/Getty Images Plus; p. 38: ferrantraite/E+; p. 39: John Fedele/Blend Images; p. 41 (C): Adrin Gmez/EyeEm; p. 41 (CR): Tim Hawley/Photographer's Choice RF; p. 42 (TR): Lilly Roadstones/Taxi; p. 42 (BR): Caiaimage/Tom Merton; p. 43: Digital Vision./Photodisc; p. 44 (walk): Inti St Clair/Blend Images; p. 44 (run): JGI/Tom Grill/Blend Images; p. 44 (work): Squaredpixels/E+; p. 44 (study): Geber86/E+; p. 44 (soccer): Thomas Barwick/Taxi; p. 47: David Stuart/Stockbyte; p. 48: Christopher Malcolm/The Image Bank; p. 49 (B): Wavebreakmedia/iStock/Getty Images Plus; p. 51: Juanmonino/E+; p. 52 (man): Jacqueline Veissid/Blend Images; p. 52 (commuters): Ovidio Ferreira/EyeEm; p. 53: David Nunuk/All Canada Photos; p. 54 (mall), p. 62 (photo c): Henglein And Steets/Photolibrary; p. 54 (store): m-imagephotography/iStock/Getty Images Plus; p. 54 (hotel): John Warburton-Lee/AWL Images; p. 54 (school): Robert Daly/Caiaimage; p. 54 (restaurant): Tom Merton/OJO Images; p. 54 (supermarket): David Nevala/Aurora; p. 54 (museum): Eric VANDEVILLE/Gamma-Rapho; p. 54 (hospital), p. 62 (photo g): Steven Frame/Hemera/Getty Images Plus; p. 54 (café): Klaus Vedfelt/Taxi; p. 54 (bookstore): M_a_y_a/E+; p. 54 (thetre): Clara Li/EyeEm; p. 54 (park), p. 62 (photo a): Eric You/EyeEm; p. 54 (zoo): John Hart/EyeEm; p.55: fotoVoyager/E+; p. 56 (1a): Aimin Tang/Photographer's Choice; p. 56 (1b): Barry Kusuma/Stockbyte; p. 56 (1c): Alan_Lagadu/iStock/Getty Images Plus; p. 56 (1d): swedewah/E+; p. 56 (1e): Witold Skrypczak/Lonely Planet Images; p. 56 (statue): Jeremy Walker/Photographer's Choice; p. 57: cinoby/E+; p. 58: JGI/Jamie Grill/Blend Images; p. 59: Julia Davila-Lampe/Moment Open; p. 60 (BG): Macduff Everton/Iconica; p. 60 (CR): Cesar Okada/E+; p. 60 (TL): Neil Beckerman/The Image Bank; p. 61 (waterfall): Kimie Shimabukuro/Moment Open; p. 61 (Christ): joSon/The Image Bank; p. 61 (flower): SambaPhoto/Cristiano Burmester/SambaPhotol; p. 61 (monkey): Kryssia Campos/Moment; p. 62 (BG): Planet Observer/UIG/Universal Images Group; p. 62 (photo b): Bernard Jaubert/Canopy; p. 62 (photo d): Caiaimage/Robert Daly/OJO+; p. 62 (photo f): Gary Yeowell/The Image Bank; p. 143 (living room): imagenavi; p. 143 (kitchen): Glasshouse Images/Corbis.

Front cover photography by Arctic-Images/The Image Bank/Getty Images.

Illustrations by: Ana Djordevic (Astound US) p. 5; Alejandro Mila (Sylvie Poggio Artists Agency) pp. 23, 30; Joanna Kerr (New Division) pp. 44, 50; Dusan Lakicevic (Beehive Illustration) pp. 24, 46.

Audio production by CityVox, New York.

EVOLVE

SPEAKING MATTERS

EVOLVE is a six-level American English course for adults and young adults, taking students from beginner to advanced levels (CEFR A1 to C1).

Drawing on insights from language teaching experts and real students, EVOLVE is a general English course that gets students speaking with confidence.

This student-centered course covers all skills and focuses on the most effective and efficient ways to make progress in English.

Confidence in teaching.
Joy in learning.

Better Learning WITH EVOLVE

Better Learning is our simple approach where insights we've gained from research have helped shape content that drives results. Language evolves, and so does the way we learn. This course takes a flexible, student-centered approach to English language teaching.

EVOLVE

STUDENT'S BOOK

Leslie Anne Hendra, Mark Ibbotson, and Kathryn O'Dell

1

CAMBRIDGE

Meet our student contributors

Videos and ideas from real students feature throughout the Student's Book.

Our student contributors describe themselves in three words.

LARISSA CASTRO

Friendly, honest, happy
Centro Universitario
Tecnológico, Honduras

JINNY LARA

Free your mind
Centro Universitario
Tecnológico, Honduras

CAROLINA NASCIMENTO NEGRÃO

Nice, determined, hard-working
Universidade Anhembi Morumbi,
Brazil

JOSUE LOZANO

Enthusiastic, cheerful, decisive
Centro Universitario
Tecnológico, Honduras

JULIETH C. MORENO DELGADO

Decisive, reliable, creative
Fundación Universitaria
Monserrate, Colombia

ANDERSON BATISTA

Resilient, happy, dreamer
Universidade Anhembi
Morumbi, Brazil

FELIPE MARTINEZ LOPEZ

Reliable, intrepid, sensitive
Universidad del Valle de
México, Mexico

JEE-HYO MOON (JUNE)

Organized, passionate, diligent
Mission College, USA

Student-generated content

EVOLVE is the first course of its kind to feature real student-generated content. We spoke to over 2,000 students from all over the world about the topics they would like to discuss in English and in what situations they would like to be able to speak more confidently.

The ideas are included throughout the Student's Book and the students appear in short videos responding to discussion questions.

INSIGHT

Research shows that achievable speaking role models can be a powerful motivator.

CONTENT

Bite-sized videos feature students talking about topics in the Student's Book.

RESULT

Students are motivated to speak and share their ideas.

"It's important to provide learners with interesting or stimulating topics."

Teacher, Mexico (Global Teacher Survey, 2017)

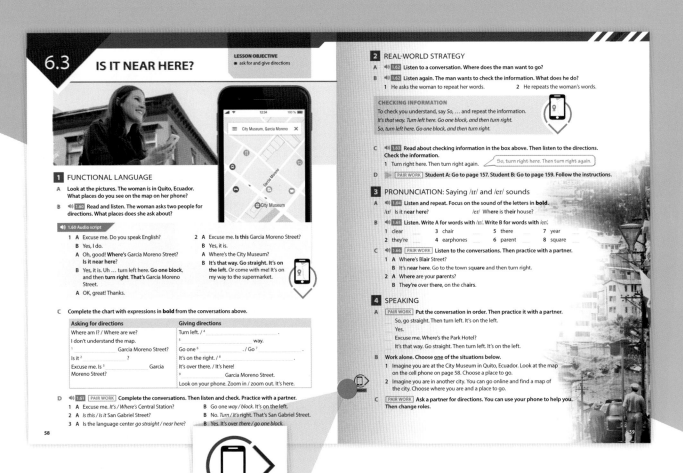

Find it

FIND IT

INSIGHT

Research with hundreds of teachers and students across the globe revealed a desire to expand the classroom and bring the real world in.

CONTENT

Find it are smartphone activities that allow students to bring live content into the class and personalize the learning experience with research and group activities.

RESULT

Students engage in the lesson because it is meaningful to them.

Designed for success

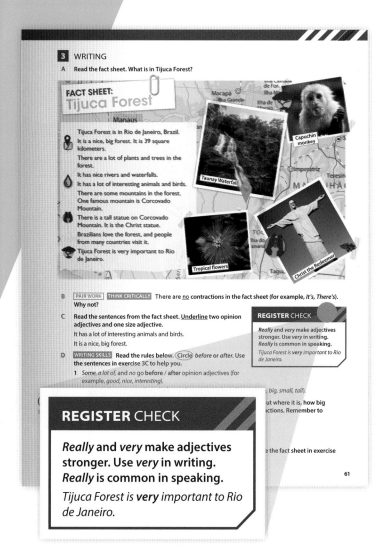

REGISTER CHECK

Really and *very* make adjectives stronger. Use *very* in writing. *Really* is common in speaking.

*Tijuca Forest is **very** important to Rio de Janeiro.*

Pronunciation

INSIGHT

Research shows that only certain aspects of pronunciation actually affect comprehensibility and inhibit communication.

CONTENT

EVOLVE focuses on the aspects of pronunciation that most affect communication.

RESULT

Students understand more when listening and can be clearly understood when they speak.

Register check

INSIGHT

Teachers report that their students often struggle to master the differences between written and spoken English.

CONTENT

Register check draws on research into the Cambridge English Corpus and highlights potential problem areas for learners.

RESULT

Students transition confidently between written and spoken English and recognize different levels of formality as well as when to use them appropriately.

6.1 GOOD PLACES

LESSON OBJECTIVE
■ talk about places in the city

1 LANGUAGE IN CONTEXT

A 🔊 1.57 Lucas and Robert are in New York City. Read and listen to their conversation. Where is Lucas from? Where is Robert from? What does Lucas want to do on Saturday?

B 🔊 1.57 Read and listen again. Are the sentences true or false?

1 Lucas has a lot of time in New York City.　　2 There is no restaurant in the hotel.

🔊 1.57 Audio script

GLOSSARY
neighborhood (n) an area of a city

Lucas I'm here, in New York City, for a week. And then I go home to Paris on Sunday.

Robert So you don't have a lot of time to see my great city.

Lucas No, I don't. There's no free time this week – it's work, work, work! But I have some time on Saturday.

Robert OK. There are a lot of places to see and things to do on the weekend. Where is your **hotel**?

Lucas It's near Central Park.

Robert No way! Central Park is great. There are some interesting museums near the **park**. Oh, and there's a **zoo** in the park!

Lucas Cool! What about places to eat? There's no **restaurant** in my hotel.

Robert Hmm … for breakfast, there's a nice **café** near here. And there are a lot of great restaurants in this neighborhood, too.

Lucas Great. Do you know some good **stores**? I don't have a lot of free time, but …

Robert Oh, yeah. There are a lot of great stores in New York. So … no museum, no park, no zoo – just shopping?

Lucas Yes!

INSIDER ENGLISH

Use *No way!* to show surprise.
No way! Central Park is great.

2 VOCABULARY: Places in cities

A 🔊 1.58 Listen and repeat the words.

bookstore　hospital　movie theater　restaurant　supermarket
café　hotel　museum　school　zoo
college　mall　park　store

B ▶ Now do the vocabulary exercises for 6.1 on page 145.

C PAIR WORK Which three places in cities do you both like? Which three <u>don't</u> you like?

54

3 GRAMMAR: There's, There are; a lot of, some, no

A (Circle) the correct answers. Use the sentences in the grammar box to help you.

1 Use *There's* with **singular / plural** nouns.
2 Use *There are* with **singular / plural** nouns.
3 Use *an / no* in negative sentences.
4 Use *some* for exact numbers / when you don't know how many things there are.

There's (= There is), There are; a lot of, some, no

There's no free time this week.	**There are** some interesting museums near the park.	**no** = zero
There's a zoo in the park.	**There are** a lot of good places to see on the weekend.	**a/an** = one
There's a nice café near here.		**some** = a small number
		a lot of = a large number

B (Circle) the correct words to complete the sentences.

1 *There's / There are* a lot of stores in the mall.
2 *There's / There are* a supermarket near the college.
3 There are *a / some* good cafés on Boston Road.
4 There's *a / a lot of* big hospital in the city.
5 There are *a lot of / no* stores, so it's great for shopping.
6 In my city, there are *a / no* zoos.

C ▶ Now go to page 134. Look at the grammar chart and do the grammar exercise for 6.1.

D Write sentences about your city. Use *there is/there are, a/an, some, a lot of,* and *no.* Then check your accuracy.

There's _____ .
There's _____ .
There are _____ .
There are _____ .
There is/are no _____ .

✓ **ACCURACY** CHECK

Use *there are, not there is,* before *a lot of* and *some* + plural noun.

There is some museums in this city. ✗
There are some museums in this city. ✓

E PAIR WORK Compare your sentences with a partner.

4 SPEAKING

PAIR WORK Talk about the things in your neighborhood. Then compare with a partner. What's the same? What's different?

There are some good restaurants near my home.

Same! And there's a movie theater near my home.

55

✓ **ACCURACY** CHECK

Use *there are*, <u>not</u> *there is*, before *a lot of* and *some* + plural noun.

There is̶ some museums in this city. ✗

There are some museums in this city. ✓

Accuracy check

INSIGHT

Some common errors can become fossilized if not addressed early on in the learning process.

CONTENT

Accuracy check highlights common learner errors (based on unique research into the Cambridge Learner Corpus) and can be used for self-editing.

RESULT

Students avoid common errors in their written and spoken English.

"The presentation is very clear and there are plenty of opportunities for student practice and production."

Jason Williams, Teacher, Notre Dame Seishin University, Japan

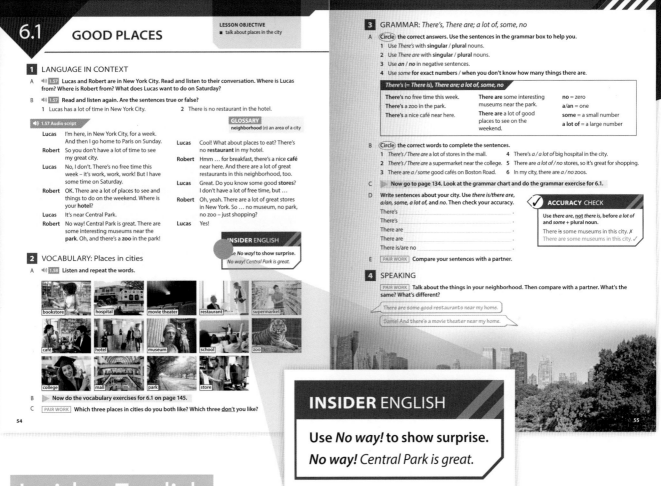

Insider English

INSIDER ENGLISH

Use *No way!* to show surprise.
No way! Central Park is great.

INSIGHT	CONTENT	RESULT
Even in a short exchange, idiomatic language can inhibit understanding.	*Insider English* focuses on the informal language and colloquial expressions frequently found in everyday situations.	Students are confident in the real world.

You spoke. We listened.

Students told us that speaking is the most important skill for them to master, while teachers told us that finding speaking activities which engage their students and work in the classroom can be challenging.

That's why EVOLVE has a whole lesson dedicated to speaking: Lesson 5, *Time to speak*.

Time to speak

INSIGHT

Speaking ability is how students most commonly measure their own progress, but is also the area where they feel most insecure. To be able to fully exploit speaking opportunities in the classroom, students need a safe speaking environment where they can feel confident, supported, and able to experiment with language.

CONTENT

Time to Speak is a unique lesson dedicated to developing speaking skills and is based around immersive tasks which involve information sharing and decision making.

RESULT

Time to speak lessons create a buzz in the classroom where speaking can really thrive, evolve, and take off, resulting in more confident speakers of English.

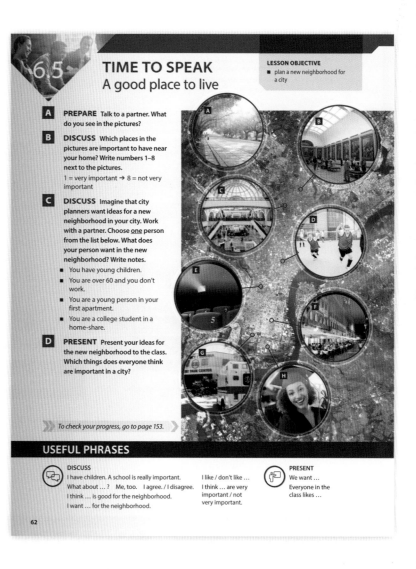

Experience Better Learning with EVOLVE: a course that helps both teachers and students on every step of the language learning journey.

Speaking matters. Find out more about creating safe speaking environments in the classroom.

EVOLVE unit structure

Unit opening page

Each unit opening page activates prior knowledge and vocabulary and immediately gets students speaking.

Lessons 1 and 2

These lessons present and practice the unit vocabulary and grammar in context, helping students discover language rules for themselves. Students then have the opportunity to use this language in well-scaffolded, personalized speaking tasks.

Lesson 3

This lesson is built around a functional language dialogue that models and contextualizes useful fixed expressions for managing a particular situation. This is a real world strategy to help students handle unexpected conversational turns.

Lesson 4

This is a combined skills lesson based around an engaging reading or listening text. Each lesson asks students to think critically and ends with a practical writing task.

Lesson 5

Time to speak is an entire lesson dedicated to developing speaking skills. Students work on collaborative, immersive tasks which involve information sharing and decision making.

CONTENTS

Functional language	Listening	Reading	Writing	Speaking
■ Check in to a hotel **Real-world strategy** ■ Check spelling		**Meet the artists** ■ Profiles of two artists	**A profile** ■ A personal or work profile ■ Capital letters and periods	■ Introduce yourself ■ Say where you're from ■ Say and spell personal information ■ Arrive at a hotel and check in **Time to speak** ■ Talk to people at a party
■ Ask about and say people's ages and birthdays; give birthday wishes **Real-world strategy** ■ Correct yourself	**Here's my band** ■ A conversation between friends		**A post** ■ A post about friends in a photo ■ *and* to join words and sentences	■ Describe the people in a picture ■ Talk about your family ■ Describe your friends and family ■ Talk about ages and birthdays **Time to speak** ■ Talk about things in common
■ Make and reply to offers **Real-world strategy** ■ Ask about words you don't understand		**A home-share in Burnaby** ■ Emails about a home-share	**An email** ■ An email about a home-share ■ Question marks	■ Describe a house in a picture ■ Talk about rooms in your home ■ Talk about unusual furniture ■ Offer a drink or snack **Time to speak** ■ Discuss what furniture to buy for a new home
■ Ask about a new topic; ask for a response **Real-world strategy** ■ Show you are listening	**Product reviews** ■ A radio program about product reviews		**A review** ■ A product review ■ *but* and *because*	■ Talk about things that you love or like ■ Talk about your favorite technology ■ Discuss what phone plan is good for you ■ Talk about how you communicate with people **Time to speak** ■ Talk about your favorite music
■ Show you agree or have things in common **Real-world strategy** ■ Short answers with adverbs of frequency		**Work, rest and play** ■ An article about work-life balance	**A report** ■ A report about your activities ■ Headings and numbered lists	■ Talk about your fun days ■ Say when and how often you do things ■ Talk about your daily routine ■ Compare information about your activities **Time to speak** ■ Talk about the best week for your body clock
■ Ask for and give directions **Real-world strategy** ■ Check information	**Walk with Yasmin** ■ A podcast about a place in nature		**A fact sheet** ■ A fact sheet ■ Order size and opinion adjectives	■ Describe a picture of a city ■ Talk about good places in your neighborhood ■ Talk about nature in your area ■ Give directions to a visitor **Time to speak** ■ Talk about a good place to live

CLASSROOM LANGUAGE

◄》 **1.02** **Get started**

Hi. / Hello.

What's your name?

My name is _____.

This is my class.

This is my partner.

This is my teacher.

Ask for help

I don't understand.

I have a question.

How do you say _____
in English?

What does _____ mean?

How do you spell _____?

Can you repeat that, please?

Sorry, what page?

Your teacher

I'm your teacher.

Open your book.

Close your book.

Go to page _____.

Do you have any questions?

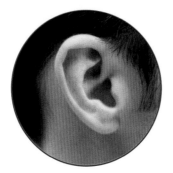

Listen.

Say.

Read.

Write.

Watch.

Work in pairs.

Work in groups.

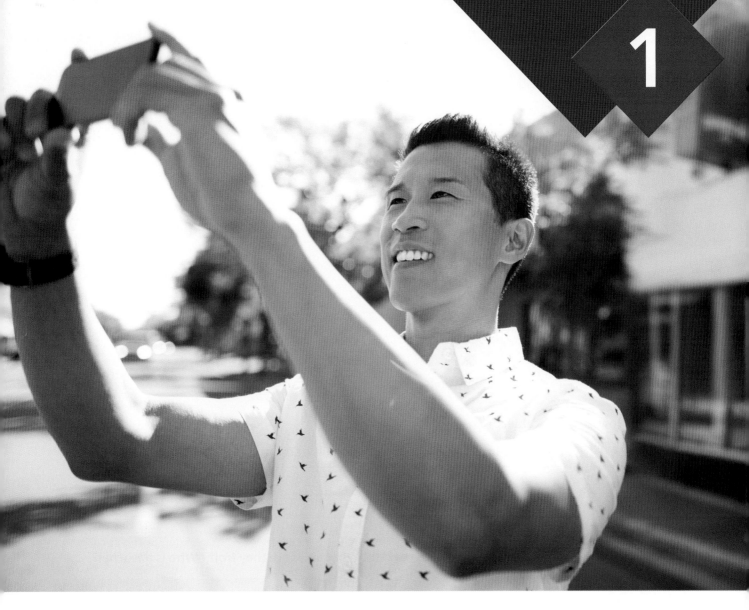

UNIT OBJECTIVES

- say where you're from
- ask for and give personal information
- check into a hotel
- write a profile
- meet new people

I AM ...

1

START SPEAKING

CLASS WORK **Say your name. Watch Josue for an example.**

I am Marco.

I am Anya.

REAL STUDENT

Where is Josue from?

1.1 I'M BRAZILIAN. AND YOU?

LESSON OBJECTIVE
- say where you're from

1 VOCABULARY: Countries and nationalities

A 1.03 **Complete the chart. Then listen and check.**

Capital city	Country	Nationality
Brasília	Brazil	1 ______
Santiago	Chile	Chilean
Beijing	China	Chinese
Bogotá	2 ______	Colombian
Quito	Ecuador	Ecuadorian
Paris	France	French
Tegucigalpa	Honduras	Honduran
Tokyo	Japan	Japanese
Mexico City	3 ______	Mexican
Lima	Peru	Peruvian
Moscow	Russia	4 ______
Seoul	South Korea	South Korean
Madrid	Spain	Spanish
Washington, D.C.	the United States	American

B **Now do the vocabulary exercises for 1.1 on page 141.**

C PAIR WORK **Talk to a partner. Say your name, nationality, and city.**

Hi! I'm Yessica. I'm Peruvian, and I'm from Callao.

Hello! I'm Daniel. I'm from Madrid, in Spain.

2 LANGUAGE IN CONTEXT

A **Read the messages from students and teachers. What cities are they from? Who is a teacher?**

International school project

Hi!

Hi, I'm Gabi. I'm **Brazilian**. I'm from **São Paulo**.

You're from **Brazil**! Wow! My name is Karina, and I'm from **Colombia**.

Are you from **Bogotá**?

No, I'm not. I'm from **Medellín**.

Write a message ...

International school project

My name is Antonio. I'm from **Mexico City** – in **Mexico**!

Hi, I'm Max. I'm **Russian**. I'm from **Moscow**.

Hi, Max. Are you a teacher?

Yes, I am. And you?

No, I'm not a teacher! I'm a student.

Write a message ...

3 GRAMMAR: *I am, you are*

A (Circle) the correct answers. Use the sentences in the grammar box to help you.

1 For questions (?), say **Are you … ?** / **You are … ?**
2 For affirmative (+) answers, say **Yes, I am.** / **Yes, I'm.**
3 For negative (-) answers, say **No, I am not.** / **No, I'm not.**

I am (= I'm), you are (= you're)		
I'm Brazilian.	**I'm not** from Lima.	**Am I** in room 6B?
You're from Mexico City.	**You're not** from Bogotá.	Yes, **you are.** / No, **you're not.**
		Are you from Tokyo?
		Yes, **I am.** / No, **I'm not.**

B Complete the sentences.

1 _____ 'm Ecuadorian.
2 Wow! _____ 're from Rio!

3 _____ you from Quito?
4 A Are you American?
    B Yes, I _____ .

C ▶ Now go to page 129. Look at the grammar chart and do the grammar exercise for 1.1.

D Look at the chart. You are Alex. Write four sentences. Then read the information in the Accuracy check box and check your work.

✓ **ACCURACY** CHECK
Use *I* with *am.*
A̶m̶ Spanish. ✗
I'm Spanish. ✓

Name	City	Nationality	Country
Alex	Orlando	American	the United States

1 _____   3 _____
2 _____   4 _____

E PAIR WORK Choose a name. Don't tell your partner. Ask and answer questions to find the person.

Harry, student New York American

Barbara, student New York Brazilian

Mike, student Chicago American

Victor, student Chicago Brazilian

Kristy, teacher New York American

Nayara, teacher New York Brazilian

Robert, teacher Chicago American

Juliano, teacher Chicago Brazilian

Are you a student?
Yes, I am.
Are you from New York?
No, I'm not. I'm from ….

4 SPEAKING

GROUP WORK Imagine you're a different person. Choose a new name, city, nationality, and country. Talk to other people. Ask questions. For ideas, watch Anderson.

REAL STUDENT

What's Anderson's city, nationality, and country?

1.2 WHAT'S YOUR LAST NAME?

LESSON OBJECTIVE
- ask for and give personal information

1 LANGUAGE IN CONTEXT

A 🔊 **1.04** **Rudy and Juana are at a conference. Listen to the conversation. Check (✓) the information they say.**

- [ ] college name
- [ ] company name
- [ ] email address
- [ ] first name
- [ ] last name (= family name)

INSIDER ENGLISH

Say *Uh-huh* to show you are listening.
My last name is Garcia. G-A-R-C-I-A.
Uh-huh. What's your email address?

B 🔊 **1.04** **Read and listen again. What information do they spell?**

🔊 **1.04 Audio script**

Rudy	So, your **first name** is Juana. H-U- …
Juana	No. J-U-A-N-A. My **last name** is Garcia. G-A-R-C-I-A.
Rudy	**Uh-huh.** What's your **email address**?
Juana	It's juanagarcia@bestmail.com.
Rudy	And what's the name of your **college**?
Juana	It's Garcia College. I'm Juana Garcia from Garcia College!

Rudy	Great! OK, my last name is Jones.
Juana	OK. What's your email address?
Rudy	It's rudythejones@kmail.com.
Juana	Rudy*the*jones! The? T-H-E?
Rudy	Yes. R-U-D-Y-T-H-E-J-O-N-E-S.
Juana	From Jones College?
Rudy	No! From Miami Dade College.

4

2 VOCABULARY: The alphabet; personal information

A 🔊 **1.05** Read and listen. Then listen again and repeat.

Aa Bb Cc **Dd** **Ee** Ff Gg Hh **Ii** Jj Kk Ll Mm
Nn **Oo** Pp **Qq** Rr Ss Tt **Uu** Vv Ww Xx Yy **Zz**

B 🔊 **1.06** Listen and circle the spelling you hear.

1	first name:	**a** Raymund	**b** Raimund	**c** Raymond
2	last name:	**a** Cummings	**b** Cummins	**c** Comyns
3	email address:	**a** cb_smith@kmail.com	**b** cg_smith@kmail.com	**c** cd_smith@kmail.com
4	college:	**a** Wallice	**b** Wallis	**c** Wallace
5	company:	**a** Jeferson	**b** Jefferson	**c** Jeffersen

C ▶ Now do the vocabulary exercises for 1.2 on page 141.

D PAIR WORK Talk to a partner. Say your first name, last name, email address, and college or company name.

> **!**
> In email addresses:
> - "." is "dot"
> - "@" is "at"
> - "_" is "underscore"

3 GRAMMAR: *What's … ?, It's …*

A Circle the correct answers. Use the sentences in the grammar box to help you.
1 For questions, say *What's … ?* / *It's …*
2 For answers, say *What's … ?* / *It's …*

> **What's …? (= What is), It's … (= It is)**
>
> **What's** your first name? **It's** Juana.
> **What's** the name of your college? **It's** Garcia College.

B Write *What's* or *It's* in the spaces. Match the questions (1–3) with the answers (a–c). Then check your accuracy.

1 _____ the name of your company? ___
2 _____ your last name? ___
3 _____ your email address? ___

a _____ luzmendes@xyz.com.
b _____ Mendes.
c _____ Warton Homes.

> ✓ **ACCURACY CHECK**
>
> Use the apostrophe (').
> ~~Whats~~ your first name? ✗
> What's your first name? ✓
> ~~Its~~ Juana. ✗
> It's Juana. ✓

C ▶ Now go to page 129. Look at the grammar chart and do the grammar exercise for 1.2.

4 SPEAKING

A Look at the information in the box. Circle three things to talk about.

college name	company name	email address	first name	last name

B CLASS WORK Talk to other people. Ask questions about the information in the box.

> *What's the name of your college?*
>
> *It's Wallace College.*

5

1.3 THIS IS THE KEY

1 VOCABULARY: Numbers

A 🔊 **1.07** **Listen and repeat the numbers.**

0	zero	**3**	three	**6**	six	**9**	nine
1	one	**4**	four	**7**	seven	**10**	ten
2	two	**5**	five	**8**	eight		

INSIDER ENGLISH

For **0**, say *zero* or *oh*.
*Your room number is two-**zero**-one.*
*My address is seven-**oh**-nine …*

B **PAIR WORK** **Say a number from exercise 1A. Your partner points to the number. Then change roles.**

2 FUNCTIONAL LANGUAGE

A 🔊 **1.08** **Paulo is at a hotel. Read and listen. Check (✓) the information the hotel clerk asks for.**

☐ cell phone number   ☐ company   ☐ name
☐ city   ☐ email address   ☐ room number

🔊 **1.08 Audio script**

Clerk Welcome to New York! What's your name?
Paulo I'm Paulo Vasques. **I'm here for three nights.**
Clerk Ah, yes. **What's your cell phone number?**
Paulo **It's (593) 555-2192.**
Clerk Thanks. And what's your email address?
Paulo It's pvasques89@travelmail.org.
Clerk Thanks. One moment. **Please sign here. Here's a pen.**

Paulo OK.
Clerk Thank you. **This is the key.** It's room 6B.
Paulo 6D. Thanks.
Clerk No, you're not in 6D. **You're in room 6B.**
Paulo Oh, OK. Thank you.
Clerk You're welcome.

B **Complete the chart with expressions in bold from the conversation above.**

Checking in (clerk)		Checking in (Paulo)
What's your ¹ _____ number? Please ² _____ here.	Here's a ³ _____ . This is the ⁴ _____ . It's room 6B. ⁵ _____ room 6B.	⁶ _____ (593) 555-2192. I'm here for three ⁷ _____ .

C 🔊 **1.09** **Complete the conversations. Then listen and check. Practice with a partner.**

1 **A** What's your *email / cell phone number*?   **B** *I'm / It's* (593) 555-3194.
2 **A** Please *sign / write* here.   **B** OK.
3 **A** Hello. Welcome to the Garden Hotel.   **B** Thanks. I'm here for two *mornings / nights*.
4 **A** *This is / It's* the key. You're in room 4D.   **B** OK. Thanks.
5 **A** *Here's a / You're* pen.   **B** Thank you.

3 REAL-WORLD STRATEGY

A 🔊 **1.10** **Listen to a conversation.** Circle **the correct answers.**

1 The woman is at *a hotel / home.*   2 She says her *room number / cell phone number.*

B 🔊 **1.10** **Read about checking spelling in the box below. Listen to the conversation again. What does the man ask the woman to spell?**

> **CHECKING SPELLING**
>
> To check spelling, ask *How do you spell your first name / your last name / it?*
> *My name is Paulo Vasques.*
> *How do you spell your last name?*
> *V-A-S-Q-U-E-S.*

C 🔊 **1.11** **Listen to the questions. Answer the questions and spell words.**

1 How do you spell your last name?   R-I-V-E-R-A.

4 PRONUNCIATION: Saying /ɪ/ and /i/ vowel sounds

A 🔊 **1.12** **Listen and repeat the two different vowel sounds.**

/ɪ/ six You're in room **6**A.   /i/ three You're in room **3**A.

B 🔊 **1.13** **Look at the** <u>underlined</u> **letters below. Then listen and repeat. What vowel sounds do you hear? Write A for words with /ɪ/, for example** *six.* **Write B for words with /i/, for example** *three.*

1	___ <u>e</u>mail	3	___ <u>i</u>nformation	5	___ k<u>e</u>y
2	___ <u>i</u>s	4	___ pl<u>ea</u>se	6	___ compan<u>y</u>

C 🔊 **1.14** PAIR WORK **Listen to the conversations.** <u>Underline</u> **words with the vowel sounds /ɪ/ and /i/. Then practice with a partner.**

1 A Is this your key?   B No, it's the key for room three.
2 A What's your company email address?   B It's c.b.smith@wallis.com.
3 A What's your Instagram name?   B It's SusieSix.

Welcome to the Tree House Hotel!

5 SPEAKING

A PAIR WORK **Put the conversation in the correct order. Then practice with a partner.**

7 A Thanks. One moment. Please sign here.

5 A Great. Thank you. And what's your email address?

☐ B I'm Marie Bernard. I'm here for two nights.

☐ B OK.

☐ B It's mbernard87@mymail.org.

☐ A Ah, yes, two nights. What's your cell phone number?

☐ B It's (298) 555-1257.

☐ A Thank you. This is the key. It's for room 7C.

1 A Hi. Welcome to the Tree House Hotel! What's your name?

B PAIR WORK **Choose a hotel in your city. One person is a hotel clerk, and the other person is a visitor. Then change roles.**

> Hi. Welcome to the International Hotel. What's your name?

> I'm Jae-hoon Park. I'm here for two nights ....

C ▶ PAIR WORK **Student A: Go to page 156. Student B: Go to page 158. Follow the instructions.**

1.4 MY PROFILE

1 VOCABULARY: Jobs

A 🔊 1.15 **Listen and repeat.**

salesperson · artist · teacher · student

hotel clerk · doctor · chef · server

2 READING

A SCAN **Read the profiles.** (Circle) **three job words from exercise 1A.**

B READ FOR DETAILS **Read the profiles again. Complete the chart.**

First name	Akemi	
Last name		Silva
City		
Nationality		
Company		
School		

C PAIR WORK **One person is Akemi. One person is Frank. How are you different?**

> I'm Akemi. I'm a student.

> I'm Frank. I'm not a student. I live in Texas …

> ❗ Use *but* to connect two different ideas.
> I'm Peruvian, **but** my home is in the United States.

> ❗ People say, *I'm from Paris.* People also say, *I **live** in Paris.* (= Paris is my home now.)

STUDIO10
STORE PROFILES
Meet the artists

ABOUT **AKEMI**

I'm Akemi Tanaka. I live in San Diego, but I'm not American. I'm Japanese. My company is Tanaka Paints. My phone number is (324) 555-6053, and my email is akemit2000@tanakapaints.com. I'm an artist, and I'm a student, too. The name of my school is The Art Institute. It's in California.

ABOUT **FRANK**

My name is Frank Silva. I live in Austin, Texas, in the United States. I'm American and Brazilian. The name of my company is Designs by Frank. It's in my home in Austin. I'm an art teacher, too. The classes are in my home. My phone number is (780) 555-5230, and my email is designsbyfrank@blinknet.com.

3 WRITING

A Read the profiles of two people. Where are they from? Who is a student?

Business Weekly

Meet the **sales team**

Lima, Peru

Hello.
My name is
Juan Carlos Fernandez.
I am Peruvian. I am from
Trujillo, but I live in Lima now.
I am a salesperson. The name of my
company is Omega Sales. My email is
jcfernandez_511@omsmail.com, and
my cell phone number is (962) 555-3198.

Class Connect –
find students around the world

Me, Katya!

Hi! I'm Katya Ivanova. I'm from Russia. My home is in St. Petersburg. It's a great city. I'm an English student. The name of my school is Popov College of English.

@ email: kativanova@popovnet.ru
🐦 Twitter: katya_ivanova98

B **PAIR WORK** **THINK CRITICALLY** The two profiles are different. Why? Discuss with a partner.

C **WRITING SKILLS** Read the rules. Then find <u>two</u> or more examples for the rules in the profiles.

Use capital letters (A, B, C ...):
- for *I* (*I'm*)
- for names of people
- for names of places, companies, schools
- for nationalities and languages
- at the beginning of sentences

 Use a period (.) at the end of statements.

 **WRITE IT**

D Choose a work profile or a personal profile. Then write your profile. Use the profiles in exercise 3A for an example.

E **GROUP WORK** Work in groups. Read other profiles. Are they work profiles or personal profiles? Say why.

TIME TO SPEAK
People from history

A   Who are the people in the pictures? Tell your partner.

B   Read the conversations (1–3). Then match them to a–c. Which conversation is with three people?

a   an introduction ___

b   a greeting ___

c   a goodbye ___

1 **A** Good evening.
    B Hello. How are you?
    A I'm fine, thanks. And you?
    B I'm fine.

2 **A** Gabi, this is Caio.
    B Hi, Gabi. Nice to meet you.
    C Nice to meet you, Caio.

3 **A** See you later.
    B Bye.

C   **PREPARE** Practice the conversations from exercise B. Then change roles.

FIND IT

D   **RESEARCH** Imagine you're at a party for people from history. Choose a person. You can go online and find the nationality and home city for your person. Create and write down a cell phone number.

E   **ROLE PLAY** Imagine you're the person from exercise D. Meet other people at the party. Write notes.

F   **AGREE** Say the nationality, city or phone number of a person from the party. Other students say the person.

G   **DISCUSS** Who is your favorite person from the party?

≫ *To check your progress, go to page 152.* ≫

USEFUL PHRASES

ROLE PLAY
Are you (American)?
Yes, I am. / No, I'm not. I'm …
I'm from (city).
How do you spell it?
A What's your cell phone number?   **B** It's …

AGREE
The person is from (city). / The phone number is …
It's (name of person).

DISCUSS
My favorite person is …
Me, too.

UNIT OBJECTIVES
- talk about your family
- describe friends and family
- talk about ages and birthdays
- write a post about friends in a photo
- compare information about friends and family

GREAT PEOPLE

2

START SPEAKING

Look at the picture. Say words about the people.

> Server.

> American.

> Family.

2.1 A FAMILY PARTY

1 LANGUAGE IN CONTEXT

A 🔊 **1.16** **Sara and Liz are at a party. Read and listen to the conversation. How old are David and Emily? Who are Elizabeth One and Elizabeth Two?**

🔊 1.16 Audio script

Sara What a great party, Liz! Are your **children** here?

Liz Yes, they are. David … He's my **son**. He's eight. And the girl with him is my daughter Emily. She's ten.

Sara And the man … Is he your **husband**?

Liz No, he's my **brother** Marcus. My husband isn't here.

Sara Oh, OK. Are your **parents** here?

Liz No, they're not. Oh, look. Here's my **grandmother**. She's 86. Grandma, this is my friend Sara.

Grandma Nice to meet you, Sara. I'm Elizabeth.

Sara Nice to meet you. Hey, are you both Elizabeth?

Liz Yes, we are! With friends, I'm Liz. But in my family, she's Elizabeth One, and I'm Elizabeth Two!

REGISTER CHECK

Some words for family are formal and informal. Use formal words at work. Use informal words with friends and family.

Formal	Informal
grandfather	*grandpa*
grandmother	*grandma*
father	*dad*
mother	*mom*

GLOSSARY

both (*det*) two people/things

2 VOCABULARY: Family; numbers

A 🔊 **1.17** **Listen and repeat the words in the family tree.**

B **Read the sentences below about Liz and her family. Then complete the family tree with the names in bold.**

- Liz = sister of **Marcus**.
- **Kyle** = uncle of Liz.
- **Tim** = cousin of Liz.
- **John** = grandfather of Liz.
- Anna = wife of **Paul**.

C 🔊 **1.18** **Complete the table with words from the family tree. Then listen and check.**

👤 Singular (1 person)	👥 Plural (2+ people)
1 _____	cousin**s**
child	2 _____
3 _____	wi**ves**

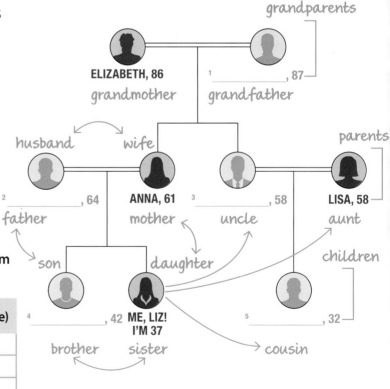

D **PAIR WORK** **Make three more sentences about the people in the family tree. Then compare with a partner.**

🔊 **1.19** **Write the numbers. Then listen and repeat.**

11 eleven	___ sixteen	21 twenty-one	___ sixty
12 twelve	___ seventeen	22 twenty-two	___ seventy
13 thirteen	___ eighteen	30 thirty	___ eighty
___ fourteen	___ nineteen	___ forty	___ ninety
___ fifteen	20 twenty	___ fifty	100 one hundred

F ▶ **Now do the vocabulary exercises for 2.1 on page 141.**

3 GRAMMAR: *is / are* in statements and *yes/no* questions

A (Circle) **the correct answers. Use the sentences in the grammar box to help you.**

1 Use **is / are** with *he* and *she*.   2 Use **is / are** with *we*, *you*, and *they*.

---
is / are in statements and *yes/no* questions

Are your children here?	**Is** he your husband?
Yes, they **are**.	No, he**'s** my brother Marcus.
He**'s** my son (**'s** = *is*). He**'s** eight.	**Are** you both Elizabeth?
She**'s** my daughter. She**'s ten**.	Yes, we **are**.

B **Complete the sentences.**

1 This _____ my sister. _____ 23.
2 **A** _____ your parents Colombian?   **B** Yes, _____ _____ .
3 This _____ my grandfather. _____ 88.
4 **A** _____ your mother at home?   **B** Yes, _____ _____ .
5 We _____ Russian. We live in Moscow.

C **Match the questions with the answers. Then answer the questions so they're true for you.**

1 Are your parents American? _b_
2 Are you 21? ___
3 Is your best friend in class? ___
4 Is your teacher Canadian? ___

a Yes. She's from Toronto.
b No. They're Colombian.
c No, he's at work.
d Yes, I am.

D ▶ **Now go to page 129. Look at the grammar chart and do the grammar exercise for 2.1.**

4 SPEAKING

A │PAIR WORK│ **Draw a simple family tree. Then talk to a partner about people in your family. Ask and answer questions. For ideas, watch Julieth.**

This is Marcos. He's from Mexico City. He's 25.

Is he your brother?

REAL STUDENT

Who does Julieth talk about? Is your family tree the same or different?

B │GROUP WORK│ **Tell your group about three people from your family tree. You can show pictures of the people on your phone.**

2.2 THEY'RE REALLY FUNNY!

1 LANGUAGE IN CONTEXT

A   Read the messages. Where is Lara from? Where is she now? Who are the other people in the pictures?

B   Read the messages again. Find the numbers in the messages. What are they?

| four | 12 | 19 | 24 | 85 |

Four days with **my family**

Hi! I'm Lara. I'm 24. I live with my family in Texas, but we're not in Texas now. We're with Grandma Vera at her home in Miami ☀️ Here's a picture of me … and here are pictures of my family 😎

Look at my mom and dad. My parents are both 50 – not **old**, and not **young**! My mom is **short** and my dad is **tall**. They're not **boring**! They're both really **funny**.

This is Erika. She's my sister – and she's my best friend! 🖤 She's 19. She's a student, and she's very **smart**. She's **shy**, but she's **friendly**, too.

This is Justin. He's my brother. He's funny. 😄 He's young (12), but he's not short – he's really **tall**.

This is my grandmother, Grandma Vera. She's old (85!), and she's very **interesting**. She's a good grandma! 🖤

2 VOCABULARY: Describing people; *really / very*

A   🔊 **1.20** Listen and repeat the adjectives below. Then find them in the messages. Match the adjectives to the people.

Age	Appearance	Personality		
old	short	boring	funny	shy
young	tall	friendly	interesting	smart

B   (Circle) *really* and *very* in the messages. Do they make the adjectives stronger (++) or weaker (--)?

C Circle the correct word to complete the sentences.

1 A Is he short?
   B No, he's not. He's *tall / shy*.

2 A Is she boring?
   B No! She's really *short / interesting*.

3 A How old is your grandmother?
   B She's 90. She's very *young / old*.

4 A Is Mi-jin a college student?
   B Yes. She's really *smart / short*.

5 A Is your cousin interesting?
   B Yes, and he's *boring / funny*.

6 A Are your children shy?
   B No, they're very *friendly / interesting*.

D ▶ **Now do the vocabulary exercises for 2.2 on page 142.**

3 GRAMMAR: *is not / are not*

A Circle the correct answers. Use the sentences in the grammar box and the Notice box to help you.

1 For negative (-) statements with *he* and *she*, use *'s not / 're not*.

2 For negative statements with *we*, *you*, and *they*, use *'s not / 're not*.

> **is not (= 's not) / are not (= 're not)**
>
> He**'s not** short.   They**'re not** boring!
> She**'s not** from Miami.   We**'re not** in Texas.
> Erika **isn't** old.   My parents **aren't** from Miami.

> **!** After pronouns (*he, she, we, you, they*), use *'s not* and *'re not*.
> She**'s not** *tall*.
> You**'re not** *from South Korea*.
> After nouns (people, places, and things), use *isn't* and *aren't*.
> Filip **isn't** *American*.
> My friends **aren't** *boring*.

B Complete the sentences with a subject (*he, she, you, we, they*) and an affirmative (+) or negative (–) verb.

1 ___He's not___ old. He's young.

2 She's friendly and really funny. _____ shy.

3 _____ from Brazil. We're not from Argentina.

4 _____ Juliana. She's Camila.

5 _____ my cousins. They're not my brothers.

6 _____ American. You're Canadian.

C ▶ **Now go to page 130. Look at the grammar charts and do the grammar exercise for 2.2.**

D PAIR WORK Write <u>two</u> true sentences and <u>two</u> false sentences about a friend or a person in your class. Then exchange sentences with a partner. Correct the false sentences.

> My friend Carina is not tall. She's very funny. She's from Japan. She's smart.

> She is very funny, and she's smart. She's tall, and she's not from Japan.

> Correct!

4 SPEAKING

A **Choose four people, for example, family or friends. Write adjectives to describe them. For ideas, watch Larissa.**

REAL STUDENT

Are your family or friends the same as Larissa's?

B GROUP WORK **Talk about your people. You can show pictures on your phone. Ask for more information about people, for example, age, nationality, and city.**

FIND IT

2.3 WHEN IS YOUR BIRTHDAY?

1 FUNCTIONAL LANGUAGE

A 🔊 1.21 **Read and listen. How many parties does Vivian talk about?**

🔊 **1.21 Audio script**

Lucas	This is a really great picture!
Vivian	Oh, thanks.
Lucas	Are they your children?
Vivian	Yes. This is Miranda. **She's eight.**
Lucas	Miranda. Nice name.
Vivian	And this is Carlos.
Lucas	**How old is he?**
Vivian	**He's three years old.**
Lucas	**When's his birthday?**

Vivian	It's March 28. **His party is on March 29.**
Lucas	Oh, right. He's four this month!
Vivian	Yeah. And **Miranda's birthday is April 2.**
Lucas	So two birthday parties in five days.
Vivian	Yeah, two parties. No, sorry, three parties! One party for Carlos, one party for Miranda, and then one party with the family.
Lucas	Well, say "**Happy birthday!**" from me!

B **Complete the chart with expressions in bold from the conversation above.**

Asking about ages and birthdays	Saying ages and birthdays	Giving birthday wishes
¹ _____ old is he?	She ³ ___ eight.	⁶ _____
When's your birthday?	He's three ⁴ _____ old.	birthday!
² _____ 's his birthday? 🧍	His party is ⁵ ___ March 29.	
When's her birthday? 🧍‍♀️	Miranda's birthday is April 2.	

2 VOCABULARY: Saying dates

A 🔊 1.22 **Look at the chart. Listen and repeat the months. What month is your birthday month?**

Months					
January	February	March	April	May	June
July	August	September	October	November	December

Dates			
1 first	7 seventh	13 thirteenth	19 nineteenth
2 second	8 eighth	14 fourteenth	20 twentieth
3 third	9 ninth	15 fifteenth	21 twenty-first
4 fourth	10 tenth	16 sixteenth	22 twenty-second
5 fifth	11 eleventh	17 seventeenth	30 thirtieth
6 sixth	12 twelfth	18 eighteenth	31 thirty-first

B 🔊 1.23 PAIR WORK **Now listen and repeat the dates. Then say the date of your birthday.**

My birthday is February eighth.

16

C   PAIR WORK   Imagine the dates below are your birthday. Work with a partner. Ask questions and say the birthdays.

1 May 8   3 August 31   5 January 25
2 November 23   4 April 19   6 June 4

When's your birthday?

It's May eighth.

3 REAL-WORLD STRATEGY

A   🔊 1.24 Listen to a conversation. (Circle) the correct answers.

1 The conversation is about a *wife / child*.
2 The man says an *age / birthday*.

B   🔊 1.24 Listen again. What number does the man say first? Then what correct number does he say?

CORRECTING YOURSELF

To correct yourself, say *No, sorry* or *Sorry, I mean …* and say the correct word.
He's twenty. No, sorry, twenty-one.
It's March twenty-first. Sorry, I mean May twenty-first.

C   Read the information in the box above about correcting yourself. What does the man say?

D   ▶   PAIR WORK   Student A: Go to page 156. Student B: Go to page 158. Follow the instructions.

4 PRONUNCIATION: Saying numbers

A   🔊 1.25 Listen and repeat the numbers. Then listen again and <u>underline</u> the stress.

13 thir<u>teen</u> / 30 <u>thir</u>ty   16 sixteen / 60 sixty   18 eighteen / 80 eighty
14 fourteen / 40 forty   17 seventeen / 70 seventy   19 nineteen / 90 ninety
15 fifteen / 50 fifty

B   PAIR WORK   Look at the numbers in the chart. Student A says a number. Student B points to the number. Then change roles.

13	80	40	18	30	60	19
70	15	17	50	90	14	16

5 SPEAKING

A   PAIR WORK   Match sentences 1–4 to sentences a–d. Then practice with a partner.

1 How old is your brother? ____
2 When's your birthday? ____
3 My brother is 30 today. ____
4 It's my birthday today. ____

a Happy birthday!
b Say "Happy birthday!" from me.
c It's June 18.
d He's 23.

B   PAIR WORK   Say the name of a friend, then say his/her birthday. Make <u>one</u> mistake. Then correct yourself.

My friend Julia. Her birthday is June fifth. No, sorry, June sixth.

HERE'S MY BAND

1 LISTENING

A [PAIR WORK] **Talk to a partner. Say what you see in the picture on page 19.**

B 🔊 **1.26** [LISTEN FOR GIST] **Listen to Isabel talk to a friend, Linda. What do they talk about?**

C 🔊 **1.26** [LISTEN FOR DETAILS] **Listen again. Circle the words that Isabel uses to describe the people.**

boring	cool	friendly	funny	interesting	shy	smart

2 GRAMMAR: Prepositions of place

A **Look at the picture on page 19 and complete the sentences with the words in the box.**

between	in	~~in~~	next to	on the left

1 We're not _____ in _____ Las Vegas! We're _____ Seattle, at college.
2 This is Joshua, on the right. And this is Nuwa, _____ .
3 I'm Isabel. Guy is _____ me.
4 Guy is _____ Nuwa and me.

3 PRONUNCIATION: Listening for short forms

A 🔊 **1.27** **Listen. Write the words you hear. Then write the full forms.**

1 ___Here's___ my band. = ___Here is___   3 _____ really funny. = _____
2 _____ in Seattle. = _____   4 _____ great! = _____

B 🔊 **1.28** **Complete the conversation with the words in the box. Listen and check.**

I'm	It's	She's	What's	When's

1 Nice to meet you, Sara. _____ Elizabeth.
2 A _____ your birthday?
  B _____ March 14.
3 This is Nuwa. _____ really smart.
4 _____ your name?

4 WRITING

A **Read the post. How old are the students?**

SOCIALHUB

JING
September 12 at 2:24pm

We're four college students in Seattle, and we're in a band. The name of the band is *JING*. Joshua is on the right. He's 22, and he's from Chicago. He's really friendly and funny. The first letter in *JING* is for Joshua. I'm Isabel. I'm 20, and I'm the "I" in the band name. I'm next to Joshua. Nuwa is on the left. She's 21. She's Chinese, and she's here for school. She's very interesting and smart. She's the "N." Guy is between Nuwa and me. He's 20, and he's the "G." He's shy, so he's the last letter in the name!

👍 Like   💬 Comment   ➡ Share

👍 35   ❤ 35

B **PAIR WORK** **THINK CRITICALLY** **Why is the name of the band "JING"? Is it a good name?**

C **WRITING SKILLS** **Read about two ways to use *and*. Match them (1–2) to the correct example sentence (a–b).**

1 Use *and* to connect words. ___

2 Use *and* to connect two sentences and make one long sentence. ___

a We're four college students in Seattle, and we're in a band.

b She's very interesting and smart.

D **Read the post again and underline examples of *and*. Does *and* connect words or sentences?**

 **WRITE IT**

E Choose a picture of you with three or four people. Write a post about the picture. Say where you are (*in* + city/country). Say where people are in the picture (*next to, on the left/right, between*). Give information about the people. Use *and* to connect words and sentences. Then check your accuracy.

 **ACCURACY CHECK**

After prepositions, use *me*, not *I*.

Guy is next to I. ✗
Guy is next to me. ✓
He's between Nuwa and I. ✗
He's between Nuwa and me. ✓

Seattle

TIME TO SPEAK
True for me

A Which family members are in the picture? Compare your ideas with a partner.

B **PREPARE** Complete the sentences so they're true for you.

1 My mom is _____ (nationality).
2 My dad is _____ (age).
3 My grandmother is _____ (name).
4 My grandfather is from _____ (city).
5 My best friend is _____ (personality).
6 My birthday is in _____ (month).

C **DISCUSS** Say your answers from exercise B. Your partner says *"True for me"* or *"Not true for me."* Then change roles.

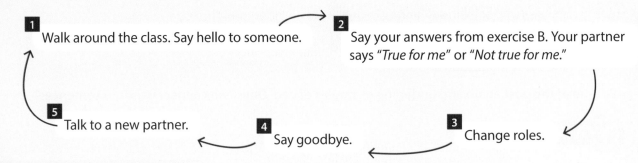

My mom is Brazilian.

Not true for me.

My dad is 50.

True for me.

D Read the instructions. Then talk to people in your class.

1 Walk around the class. Say hello to someone.

2 Say your answers from exercise B. Your partner says *"True for me"* or *"Not true for me."*

3 Change roles.

4 Say goodbye.

5 Talk to a new partner.

E **PRESENT** Who has the same answers? Who has different answers? Tell the class.

To check your progress, go to page 152.

USEFUL PHRASES

  DISCUSS
Hello./Hi.   My name is …
True for me.   Not true for me.
Really? (for surprise) Goodbye.

  PRESENT
(Name) is the same.
(Name) is different.

UNIT OBJECTIVES

■ talk about your home
■ talk about furniture
■ offer and accept a drink and snack
■ write an email about a home-share
■ choose things for a home

COME IN

3

START SPEAKING

A **Look at the picture. Where is this house?**

B **Who is in the house?**

C **What is in the house?**

WELCOME TO MY HOME

LESSON OBJECTIVE
- talk about your home

wall · bedroom

window · bathroom

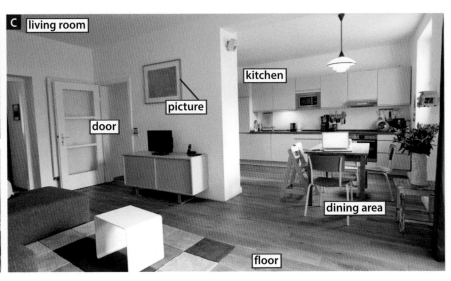

living room · kitchen · picture · door · dining area · floor

1 VOCABULARY: Rooms in a home

A 🔊 1.29 **Listen and repeat the words in the pictures. Which words are rooms? Which words are things in rooms?**

B **PAIR WORK** **Talk to a partner. What's your favorite room in the pictures?**

C ▶ **Now do the vocabulary exercises for 3.1 on page 142.**

2 LANGUAGE IN CONTEXT

A 🔊 1.30 **Alina gives a video tour of her family's home. Listen and read. How many rooms does she talk about?**

  a six   b seven   c eight

B 🔊 1.30 **Listen again. Answer the questions.**

1 What is on the wall?
2 Who is in the kitchen?
3 How many bathrooms are in the apartment?
4 What are the names of the cat and the dog?

C **PAIR WORK** **What are your favorite rooms? Talk to a partner. For ideas, watch Felipe's video.**

REAL STUDENT *What are Felipe's favorite rooms? Are your favorite rooms the same?*

Hi! Welcome to my new home. I mean, my *family's* new home. We live in an apartment, not a house. OK. First, this is the **living room**, with my mom's favorite **picture** on the **wall**. And this is the **dining area**. It's good for family dinners, or pizza with my friends. And this is the **kitchen**, through the **door**! My mom and her friend are in there now. OK, and this is the **bathroom**, the family bathroom. And here, this is my parents' **bedroom**, with a second bathroom. And this is my bedroom, with two **windows**. Oh! This is Milka. She's our cat. And this is Sergei's room. He's my brother. Hey! T-Rex is on Sergei's bed! Bad dog! On the floor! Now! T-Rex is Sergei's dog. OK, now say "hi" to the camera, T-Rex. Welcome to our apartment!

✓ ACCURACY CHECK

Use *the* when you talk about a specific thing in your home: *the floor* in *the kitchen*, *the window* (in my room), or *the picture* on *the wall*.

3 GRAMMAR: Possessive adjectives; possessive 's and s'

A **(Circle) the correct answers. Use the sentences in the grammar box and the Notice box below to help you.**

1 The *'s* in *Sergei's room* = **possession** / *is*.
2 Possessive adjectives (for example, *my, our, his* …) go **before** / **after** a noun.
3 Add *'s* to **singular** / **plural** nouns.
4 Add an apostrophe (') after *s* of a **singular** / **plural** noun.

Possessive adjectives; possessive 's and s'

Welcome to **my** home.	This is **your** bedroom.
This is **her** bedroom.	This is **his** bedroom.
This is **their** bedroom.	This is my parents' bedroom.
Milka is **our** cat.	T-Rex is Sergei**'s** dog.
This is my apartment. **Its** windows are old, but **its** doors are new.	

! a **noun** = a person or thing, for example, *Katya* or *room*.
Singular nouns are **1 thing**.
Plural nouns are **2+ things**.

B **Complete the sentences. Use the possessive form of the word in parentheses ( ).**

1 Is _____your_____ (you) apartment in the city?
2 It's not _____ (my parents) bedroom.
3 What's _____ (John) last name?
4 Maria is _____ (he) wife.

5 _____ (We) home is in Santiago.
6 The _____ (cat) name is Milka.
7 _____ (They) daughter is a college student.
8 What's _____ (she) email address?

C ▶ **Now go to page 130. Look at the grammar charts and do the grammar exercise for 3.1.**

D **PAIR WORK** **Complete the sentences with information about you. Then compare with a partner.**

> My *dog's* name is Friday.

1 _____ name is _____ .
2 _____ last name is _____ .
3 _____ is my best friend. _____ home is in _____ .
4 My _____ home is great. _____ living room is really interesting.
5 _____ is my cousin. The name of _____ company is _____ .

4 SPEAKING

A **Draw a plan of your home, with all the rooms.**

B **GROUP WORK** **Talk about the rooms in your homes.**

> This is my apartment. This is the door. And this is the living room, with two windows. This is my bedroom.

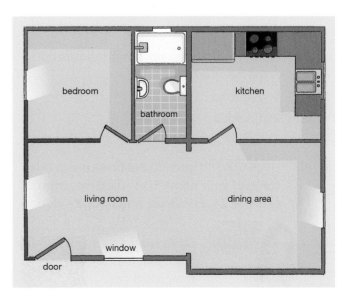

<table>
<tr><td>3.2</td><td colspan="2">## IS IT REALLY A CHAIR?</td><td>**LESSON OBJECTIVE**
■ talk about furniture</td></tr>
</table>

1 VOCABULARY: Furniture

A 🔊 **1.31** **Listen and repeat the words. Then complete the chart below. Some furniture is in more than one room.**

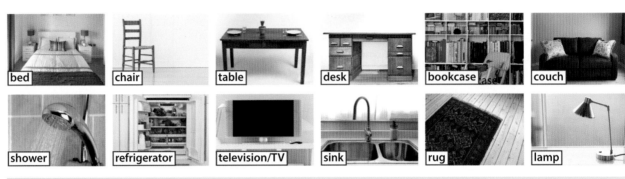

bed chair table desk bookcase couch

shower refrigerator television/TV sink rug lamp

Bedroom	Living room	Dining area	Kitchen	Bathroom
bed				

B **PAIR WORK** **Work with a partner. Say furniture from exercise 1A. Your partner says where it is in his/her home.**

> A table.

> In the kitchen. And in the living room.

C ▶ **Now do the vocabulary exercises for 3.2 on page 143.**

2 LANGUAGE IN CONTEXT

A **PAIR WORK** **Choose words to describe the picture in the article.**

big	boring	cool	funny
great	interesting	new	nice
old	small		

B **Read the article again. What room/rooms is the furniture for?**

1 A is for a _____.
2 B is for a _____.
3 C is for a _____.

C **PAIR WORK** **Describe the furniture in one room of your home. Use adjectives from exercise 2A. For ideas, watch June's video.**

REAL STUDENT

Do you and June talk about the same room and furniture?

NO **SPACE?** NO **PROBLEM!**

Is your house or apartment small? Is it *really* small? No space for big furniture? No problem! It's time for smart furniture …

A This **desk** isn't just a desk. It's a desk and a **bed**. It's great for college students.

B Is this one **chair**? Or two chairs? It's both! It's one big chair for you, or it's two small chairs for you and a friend.

C Is your living room small? No dining area in your home? This **couch** and **table** are good for a small space. First, it's a nice table for dinner. Then it's a couch!

24

3 GRAMMAR: *It is*

A (Circle) **the correct answers. Use the sentences in the grammar box to help you.**

1 Use *It's* and *It's not* for a **man or woman / thing**.

2 To make a question with *It is*, say **Is it … ? / It's … ?**

> **It is in statements and yes/no questions**
>
> | | |
> |---|---|
> | **It's** a desk and a bed. | **Is it** *really* small? |
> | **It's not** one chair, **it's** two chairs! | Yes, **it is**. |
> | | No, it **isn't**. |

B **Complete the sentences. Then match 1–4 with a–d.**

1 **A** Their house isn't old. _____ new. ___

2 **A** Where's Toronto? _____ in the United States? ___

3 **A** We're in your kitchen. _____ really cool. ___

4 **A** Where's your desk? _____ in your living room? ___

a **B** Thanks. _____ small, but it's really nice.

b **B** No, _____ . _____ in Canada.

c **B** No, _____ . _____ in my bedroom.

d **B** Oh. _____ a big or small house?

C ▶ **Now go to page 131. Look at the grammar chart and do the grammar exercise for 3.2.**

D PAIR WORK **Write an affirmative (+) and negative (–) sentence for the rooms and furniture below. Then compare with a partner.**

My TV is in my bedroom. It's not new, but it's OK.

1 my TV _____

2 my desk _____

3 my refrigerator _____

4 my bedroom _____

5 my kitchen _____

4 SPEAKING

A **Design something for the home. Use the ideas below or your ideas. Draw a picture or find a picture online.**

| an interesting lamp | a big rug | a great shower | a cool desk | a TV for the wall |

B PAIR WORK **Look at your partner's picture. Guess what it is. Is it cool? Is it interesting?**

> Is it a lamp? | Yes, it is.

25

3.3 COFFEE OR TEA?

LESSON OBJECTIVE
■ offer and accept a drink and snack

1 VOCABULARY: Drinks and snacks

A 🔊 **1.32** Listen and repeat the words. Which things are drinks? Which thing is a snack?

coffee

milk

sugar

a cookie

tea

2 FUNCTIONAL LANGUAGE

A 🔊 **1.33** Adam offers a drink and snack to his friend James. Read and listen. Which drink and snack from exercise 1A does James choose?

> **INSIDER** ENGLISH
>
> Use *sure* in informal speech to say *yes*.
> **Sure**. *A cookie, please.*
> <u>Don't</u> say *Sure, please*.

🔊 **1.33** Audio script

Adam	Coffee or tea?
James	Coffee, please.
Adam	With milk?
James	No, thanks.
Adam	OK … Here you are.
James	Thanks. Wow, this is a big cup!
Adam	It is! **Sugar?**
James	Yes, please.
Adam	One? Two?

James	In that cup? Six! No. Two, please.
Adam	Just two. And …
James	Ah! Cookies! Hmm …
Adam	They *are* small!
James	Next to the big cup, yeah – they're really small! But sure. **A cookie, please.**
Adam	Here you are!
James	Thank you.

B Complete the chart with expressions in **bold** from the conversation above.

Making offers		Replying to offers	
Coffee ¹_____ tea?		Coffee, ³_____ .	
²_____ milk?		⁴_____ , thanks.	
Sugar?		⁵_____ , please.	

3 REAL-WORLD STRATEGY

A 🔊 **1.34 Listen to a conversation. What does the man want?**

coffee ☐   tea ☐   milk ☐   sugar ☐   a cookie ☐

B 🔊 **1.34 Listen again. Circle the word the man doesn't understand. What does it mean?**

| biscuit | coffee | cookie | tea |

ASKING ABOUT WORDS YOU DON'T UNDERSTAND

To ask about a word, say *Sorry, I don't understand. What's a (word)?*
Sorry, I don't understand. What's a biscuit?

C **Read the information on asking about words you don't understand in the box above. Answer the questions.**

1 What does the man say when he doesn't understand?

2 How does he ask about the word?

4 PRONUNCIATION: Saying /k/ at the start of a word

A 🔊 **1.35 Listen and repeat. Focus on the /k/ sound.**

1 **C**offee or tea?   2 This is a big **c**up!   3 A **c**ookie, please.

B 🔊 **1.36 Listen. Which speaker (A or B) says the /k/ sound? Write A or B.**

1 coffee ___   3 kitchen ___   5 couch ___

2 cookie ___   4 cup ___   6 cool ___

C [PAIR WORK] **Work with a partner. Say the words in exercise 4B.**
Does your partner say the English /k/ sound?

5 SPEAKING

[PAIR WORK] **Work with a partner. One person is A. The other person is B.**
Then change roles.

A Offer your partner a drink/snack from exercise 1A.

B Ask about a word: "Sorry, I don't understand. What's (a) … ?"

A Point to a picture of the word on page 26: "This is (a) … ."

B Say "Yes, please." or "No, thanks."

3.4 HOME-SHARE

LESSON OBJECTIVE
- write an email about a home-share

1 READING

A SCAN Francisco is a student. He's in Burnaby in Canada for a year. He wants a room in a home-share. Scan the ad. Who is the owner of the house?

B READ FOR MAIN IDEAS Read the emails. What does Francisco ask questions about?

Home-share in Burnaby « Back to results

One bedroom, with furniture, in a five-bedroom house. Great for a student. Fifteen minutes from Morden College. No pets. From March 1. $650 a month. Contact: John Redmond at jredmond@bestmail.com

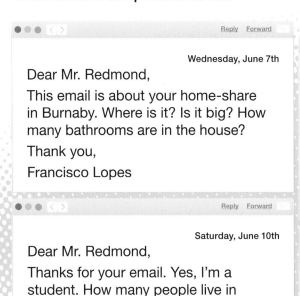

Reply Forward

Wednesday, June 7th

Dear Mr. Redmond,

This email is about your home-share in Burnaby. Where is it? Is it big? How many bathrooms are in the house?

Thank you,

Francisco Lopes

Reply Forward

Friday, June 9th

Dear Mr. Lopes,

The house is on Grafton Street in Burnaby. It's very big, with two bathrooms. One bathroom is next to the kitchen and one bathroom is next to the bedroom in my ad. Are you a student?

Sincerely,

John Redmond

Reply Forward

Saturday, June 10th

Dear Mr. Redmond,

Thanks for your email. Yes, I'm a student. How many people live in the house? Who are they? How old are they?

Thank you,

Francisco

Reply Forward

Sunday, June 11th

Dear Mr. Lopes,

Four people live in the house now. Two are students. They are 20 and 22 years old. Two are not students. Mr. Johnson is 36 years old, and Mrs. Smith is 71. She is my wife's mother.

Sincerely,

John

2 GRAMMAR: Information questions with *be*

A PAIR WORK Complete the questions with question words from the emails in exercise 1B. Then find John's answers to the questions. Use the questions and answers to have a conversation with a partner.

1 _____ is it?

2 _____ _____ bathrooms are in the house?

3 _____ _____ people live in the house?

4 _____ are they?

5 _____ _____ are they?

B ▶ Now go to page 131. Look at the grammar chart and do the grammar exercise for 3.4.

C PAIR WORK THINK CRITICALLY Is this a good place for Francisco to live? Why or why not?

28

Home-share on **BOND STREET**

✉ **Contact owner**

3 WRITING

A   **Francisco writes to the owner of a second home-share. Read the emails. Answer the questions.**

1   Is the owner a woman or a man?

2   How many questions are about the house? the people?

3   Look at the pictures above. Which rooms do you see? Which room is in the email but isn't in the pictures?

4   Is it a good place for Francisco? Why or why not?

Reply Forward

Dear Mrs. Hyland,

This email is about your home-share in Burnaby. Where is it? How many bedrooms and bathrooms are in it? How many people are in the house? Are they students? I'm a student at Morden College, and I'm 22.

Thank you,

Francisco Lopes

Reply Forward

Dear Mr. Lopes,

Thank you for your email. The house is on Bond Street. It's big, with four bedrooms, three bathrooms, and a big kitchen. Three people live in the house now. They are students at Morden College. They are your age – 22.

Sincerely,

Emma Hyland

B   **WRITING SKILLS** ⟨Circle⟩ the question marks (?) in Francisco's email, above. Then ⟨circle⟩ the correct answer in the rules, below.

1   Use **one question mark / two question marks** for each question.

2   The question mark is at **the end / the beginning** of each question.

 **WRITE IT**

C   Write an email to the owner of a home-share. Start with: *This email is about …* Ask questions about the house and the people.

D   PAIR WORK   Exchange emails with a partner. Write a reply to your partner. Write about a bad place or a good place.

E   PAIR WORK   Read your partner's reply. Is it a good place or a bad place?

TIME TO SPEAK
A new home

Hi, I'm Jason. I'm 25 years old. I'm single, and I'm a student. I ♥ soccer and parties. This is my new apartment!

A **DISCUSS** Talk about Jason's new home with a partner. Say the rooms you see. Is it a good home for him?

B **PREPARE** Talk about the things in the pictures. Which rooms are good places for them?

A $120	B $180	C $150	D $80	E $30
F $60	G $280	H $330	I $80	J $120
K $20	L $60	M $10	N $10	O $10

C **DECIDE** With a partner, make a list of things to buy for Jason's new home. You have $1,000.

D **PRESENT** Compare your lists. Which list is the class' favorite?

To check your progress, go to page 152.

USEFUL PHRASES

 DISCUSS
This is the (kitchen/…)
It's good for him. / It's not good for him.

 PREPARE
Where's a good place for a (couch/…)?
In the living room?

 DECIDE
What's important for Jason?
This is a big/small (TV).
It's $180 ($ = dollars).
It's expensive. ($$$)
It's cheap. ($)

What about this (TV/…)?
This TV is good for Jason.
I agree. / I don't agree.
Good idea!

REVIEW 1 (UNITS 1–3)

1 VOCABULARY

A Write the words in the correct place in the chart.

artist	chef	French	Mexico	server
bookcase	Colombia	Honduran	parents	South Korea
~~Brazil~~	cousin	hotel clerk	Peruvian	table
brother	desk	Japanese	refrigerator	wife

Countries	Nationalities	Jobs	Family	Furniture
Brazil				

B Write <u>one</u> more word for the categories in exercise 1A.

2 GRAMMAR

A Complete the sentences with the words in the box.

're not	's	's	Are	I'm not	Is	isn't	it is

1 Loretta _____ friendly. She's nice, too.

2 A _____ you shy?   B No, _____ .

3 Donna _____ 14. She's only 13.

4 What _____ your last name?

5 They _____ from Chicago. They're from Dallas.

6 A _____ your company in China?   B Yes, _____ .

B (Circle) the correct answers.

¹ My / I name is Sam, and this is Vic. We're brothers. This is ² their / our apartment. ³ Vic / Vic's room is big. ⁴ My / His room is small, but it's OK. It's next to the kitchen! We're in apartment 22B. ⁵ We / Our sister and ⁶ her / his husband are in apartment 23B.

C Write <u>five</u> things about your home and family. Use possessive adjectives and possessive 's/s'.

3 SPEAKING

A PAIR WORK Think of a person you <u>and</u> your partner know. Think about the person's job, age, nationality, and other information. Describe the person. Your partner guesses the person. Then change roles.

> She's a student. She's 21. She's our friend. She's Peruvian. She's very funny.

> Is it Alessa?

B Write two sentences about your partner's person.

4 FUNCTIONAL LANGUAGE

A ⊙ the correct answers to complete the conversation.

Teacher Welcome to the college language center. What's your name?

Sabrina It's Sabrina Calvo.

Teacher How do you ¹ *spell / mean* your last name?

Sabrina C-A-L-V-O.

Teacher Thank you. OK. ² *How / When* old are you, and ³ *how's / when's* your birthday?

Sabrina I'm ⁴ *21 / 21st*. My birthday ⁵ *is / are* August 2.

Teacher OK. You're ⁶ *on / in* room 6C. Sorry, I ⁷ *spell / mean* room 6D. It's next to the library.

Sabrina Sorry, I don't ⁸ *understand / mean*. ⁹ *Where's / What's* a library?

Teacher It's a room with books.

Sabrina OK. Thank you.

B Complete the conversation with the words in the box. There is <u>one</u> extra word.

milk	please	tea	thanks	yes

Server Coffee or ¹_____ ?

Ivan Tea, ²_____ .

Server OK. With ³_____ ?

Ivan No, ⁴_____ .

5 SPEAKING

A PAIR WORK Choose <u>one</u> of the situations below. Talk to a partner. Have a conversation.

1 You are at a hotel. A clerk asks for your personal information. Answer the questions. Look at page 6 for useful language.

> Good evening. Welcome to Hotel 24. What's your name?

2 You ask a friend about his/her family's ages and birthdays. Your friend answers your questions. Look at page 16 for useful language.

> Is this your daughter? How old is she?

3 A friend is at your home. Offer him or her a drink and a snack. Look at page 26 for useful language.

> Coffee or tea?

B PAIR WORK Change roles and repeat the situation.

UNIT OBJECTIVES

■ talk about your favorite things
■ say how you use technology
■ talk about how you communicate
■ write product reviews
■ talk about your favorite music

I LOVE IT

4

START SPEAKING

A Look at the people in the picture. Where are they? Why are they here?

B Talk about things you like 🙂 or love ❤. For ideas, watch the video with June and Felipe.

REAL STUDENTS

What do June and Felipe like or love?

33

FAVORITE THINGS

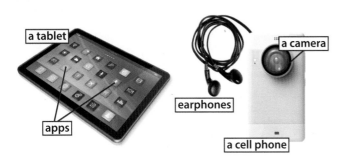

a tablet

apps

earphones

a cell phone

a camera

a game

a laptop

a smartwatch

1 VOCABULARY: Technology

! **A laptop is a computer.**

A 🔊 1.37 **Look at the pictures above. Listen and repeat the words.**

B PAIR WORK **Look at the pictures again. Which things do you like? Which things don't you like? Tell a partner.**

😊 I like this.   ☹ I don't like this.

C ▶ **Now do the vocabulary exercises for 4.1 on page 143.**

2 LANGUAGE IN CONTEXT

A **Read the webpage. What things from exercise 1A do the people talk about? Which thing on the webpage isn't in the pictures above?**

zozo **I love my refrigerator. Am I OK?**

COMMENTS

JJ	You love a refrigerator! No, you're not OK! We love people – we don't love things.
erico–hello	I don't agree, JJ! I love my family … and I love my smartwatch. We love people, *and* we love things.
vera	True. I love my cell phone and the apps on it. I don't have a tablet, but I really want an iPad. Yes, it's OK to love things. But a *refrigerator*? I have a nice refrigerator. I *like* it, but I don't *love* it.
stee33	I don't love my refrigerator, but I love the things in it! 😊

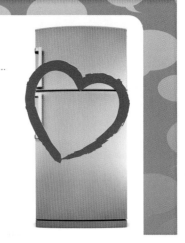

B **Read the webpage again. Are sentences 1–6 true or false for the people? ⃝Circle the correct answer.**

1 I have a refrigerator.   For zozo, this is *true* / *false*.
2 I love things.   For erico-hello, this is *true* / *false*.
3 I have a tablet.   For vera, this is *true* / *false*.
4 I want a tablet.   For vera, this is *true* / *false*.
5 I have a cell phone with apps.   For vera, this is *true* / *false*.
6 I love my refrigerator.   For stee33, this is *true* / *false*.

3 GRAMMAR: Simple present statements with *I, you, we*

A ⟨Circle⟩ the correct answers. Use the sentences in the grammar box to help you.

1 Use the simple present for things that are **generally true** / **finished**.

2 Use *I, you,* or *we* / *I'm, you're,* or *we're* with present simple verbs.

3 Use *don't* in **affirmative** / **negative** simple present statements.

4 Simple present verbs have **the same** / **different** spelling after *I, you,* and *we*.

Simple present statements with *I, you, we*	
I **love** my watch.	I **don't love** my refrigerator.
I **have** a cell phone.	I **don't have** a tablet.
You **want** a tablet.	You **don't want** a watch.
We **love** our family.	We **don't love** things.

B Complete the sentences with the words in the box.

don't have	don't like	don't want	have	love	want

1 My new smartwatch is cool.
I _____ it!

2 I _____ my
earphones. They aren't very good.

3 I _____ 85 apps on
my cell phone.

4 We _____ games
on our cell phones. We don't like them.

5 I don't like tablets. I don't have a tablet,
and I _____ a tablet.

6 Your laptop is really old. You
_____ a new laptop.

C ▶ **Now go to page 131. Look at the grammar chart and do the grammar exercise for 4.1.**

Now go to page 131. Look at the grammar chart and do the grammar exercise for 4.1.

D PAIR WORK Complete the sentences. Make them true for you. Then compare with a partner.

1 I _____ a smartwatch.

2 I _____ my cell phone.

3 I _____ games on
my cell phone.

4 I _____ tablets.

5 I _____ a new
computer.

4 SPEAKING

PAIR WORK **What technology do you have? What do you love? What don't you like? Tell your partner. For ideas, watch Anderson's video.**

> I have a good app. It's KickMap. I love it.

> I like iPhones. I want a ...

REAL STUDENT

*Do you have the
same things?*

35

4.2 MY PHONE IS MY WORLD

1 LANGUAGE IN CONTEXT

A 🔊 **1.38** **Read and listen. Olivia is at a phone store, TechUBuy.** (Circle) **the things she talks about.**

family	friends	her laptop	her phone	school	work

GLOSSARY

phone plan (*n*) a service you pay for to make calls, send messages, and use the internet on your cell phone

🔊 **1.38 Audio script**

Clerk Welcome to TechUBuy!

Olivia Hi! I want a new phone plan. I love my phone. It's my world! But my plan is expensive.

Clerk Do you know which plan you want?

Olivia No. I have no idea.

Clerk OK. First, I have some questions. What do you do on your phone? Do you **call** your friends?

Olivia No. I **chat** with my friends, but I don't *call* them. We **send messages**. And we **leave voice messages**.

Clerk Ah, yes. And do you **send emails**?

Olivia Yes. I **read emails** on my phone – from friends and for work.

Clerk And what else? Do you **listen to music** on your phone?

Olivia Yes, I do, and I **watch videos**. I also **use social media** – I **post photos**, **leave comments**, …

Clerk OK. Your phone really *is* your world! So, we have three phone plans …

2 VOCABULARY: Using technology

A **Read the chart. Which verbs are <u>not</u> in the conversation in exercise 1A?**

INSIDER ENGLISH

Say *What else?* to ask for more information about a topic.
*And **what else?** Do you listen to music on your phone?*

verbs + nouns		
buy apps / games / music / movies	**play** games	**leave** voice messages / comments
call friends / family	**post** photos / comments	**use** apps / social media / technology
chat with friends / family	**read** emails / messages	
listen to music	**send** emails / (text) messages	**watch** movies / videos / TV
… on the internet … on my computer / laptop … on my cell phone / tablet … on my smartwatch		

| I call family on my cell phone. | I listen to music on my phone. | I chat with friends on the internet. | I use apps on my cell phone and tablet. | I play games on my computer. | I read emails on my tablet. | I send text messages on my phone. | I post photos on the internet. |

B 🔊 **1.39** **Look at the pictures. Listen and repeat. Then say <u>three</u> things you do.**

C ▶ **Now do the vocabulary exercises for 4.2 on page 144.**

36

3 GRAMMAR: Simple present *yes/no* questions with *I, you, we*

A **(Circle) the correct answers. Use the sentences in the grammar box to help you.**

1 To make simple present questions, use **Do / Are** + the subject (for example, *I* or *we*) + a verb.

2 To make negative short answers, use **do / don't**.

Simple present *yes/no* questions with *I, you, we*	
Do I **post** good photos?	Yes, you **do**. / No, you **don't**.
Do you **use** social media?	Yes, I **do**. / No, I **don't**.
Do you **know** which plan you want?	Yes, I **do**. / No, I **don't**.
Do you and your friends **send** emails?	Yes, we **do**. / No, we **don't**.

B **Complete the *yes/no* questions. Use the words in parentheses ( ).**

1 _____ on your computer? (*you, listen to music*)

2 _____ on your phone? (*you, play games*)

3 _____ to your teachers? (*you and your friends, send text messages*)

4 _____ on social media? (*you, post comments*)

5 _____ on your laptop? (*you, watch videos*)

C PAIR WORK **Ask and answer the questions so they are true for you. Say "Yes, I do." or "No, I don't."**

D ▶ **Now go to page 132. Look at the grammar chart and do the grammar exercise for 4.2.**

4 SPEAKING

A PAIR WORK **What do you do on your phone and the internet? Compare with a partner.**

B PAIR WORK **Look at the cell phone plans. Which plan is good for you? Why? Ask and answer questions with a partner. Use the conversation on page 36 to help you.**

Do you play games on your phone?

No, I don't. I call friends and family, and I send text messages. I don't use social media on my phone. Plan 1 is good for me.

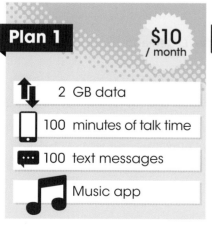

Plan 1 — $10 / month

- 2 GB data
- 100 minutes of talk time
- 100 text messages
- Music app

Plan 2 — $15 / month

- 5 GB data
- 50 minutes of talk time
- 200 text messages
- Photo app

Plan 3 — $20 / month

- 10 GB data
- 60 minutes of talk time
- 50 text messages
- 5 games

4.3

WHAT ABOUT YOU?

1 FUNCTIONAL LANGUAGE

A **PAIR WORK** How do you communicate with family and friends? Check (✓) the things you use. Then compare with your partner.

- ☐ cards
- ☐ email
- ☐ letter
- ☐ phone
- ☐ social media
- ☐ video chat

B 🔊 **1.40** Rocío, a college student in Los Angeles, talks to her new friend Jeff. Read and listen. How do they communicate with family and friends?

🔊 **1.40 Audio script**

Jeff	So, you're from Chile. Does your family live in Chile, too?
Rocío	Yes, but LA is my home now! I use technology to chat with my family. I call my parents on my phone, and I send messages to my brothers. It's really nice.
Jeff	Right. **What about email?**
Rocío	Yeah. I send emails to my friends in Chile. **How about you?**
Jeff	I like email, but I use Facebook, too.

Rocío	OK. I like Instagram.
Jeff	Oh, yeah? **Do you post photos?**
Rocío	Yes, photos of LA. My family and friends really like them. **Do you post photos, too?**
Jeff	No, but I post comments on other people's photos.
Rocío	Nice comments?
Jeff	Yes, of course!

C Complete the chart with expressions in **bold** from the conversation above.

Asking about a new topic	Asking for a response
1 _____ email?	3 _____ post photos,
2 _____ post photos?	4 _____ ?
Do you send cards? / use social media?	5 _____ about you?
	What about you?
	And you?

D 🔊 **1.41** **PAIR WORK** Put the conversations in the correct order. Listen and check. Then practice with a partner.

1 ___ Yes, I do. Do you use it, too?
  ___ Yes, it is. I really like it.
  _1_ Do you use Instagram?
  ___ No. Is it interesting?

2 ___ No, but I send birthday messages.
  ___ Yes, to my family and friends. What about you?
  ___ Hmm … birthday messages are OK, but I like cards.
  _1_ Do you send birthday cards to your family?

2 REAL-WORLD STRATEGY

SHOWING YOU ARE LISTENING
To show you are listening, say *Right*, *Yeah*, or *OK*.
Jeff   *I use Facebook, too.*
Rocío   *OK. I like Instagram.*

A   Read about how to show you are listening in the box above. What does Rocío say?

B   ◀ﮩ 1.42 Listen to a conversation. How does the man communicate with his family?

C   ◀ﮩ 1.42 Listen again. What does the woman say to show she's listening?

D   ▶ PAIR WORK Student A: Go to page 156. Student B: Go to page 159. Follow the instructions.

3 PRONUNCIATION: Saying stressed words

A   ◀ﮩ 1.43 Listen and repeat the questions. Which words are stressed? Why are they stressed?

   1 What about email?   **2** How about you?   **3** Do you post photos?

B   ◀ﮩ 1.44 Listen and <u>underline</u> the stressed words in the questions.

   A Do you use Facebook? (1 word)

   B Yeah. How about you? (1 word)

   A Me, too. I post photos and comments.

   B Do you post videos? (2 words)

   A No, but I send videos on WhatsApp.

   B Do you use video chat? (2 words)

   A Yeah, video chat is great.

C   PAIR WORK Practice the conversation in exercise 3B. Does your partner use stressed words?

4 SPEAKING

A   Think about ways to communicate with people. Which ways do you use? Write a list.

B   PAIR WORK Talk to a partner about how you communicate. Ask questions to start a new topic. Show you are listening.

> I use Instagram. It's great.

> Yeah.

> Do you use Instagram, too?

> Yes, and I use Snapchat. What about you?

> I don't use Snapchat.

4.4 GREAT! FIVE STARS

1 LISTENING

A **PAIR WORK** **Read the definition of "product review." Then answer the questions with a partner.**

1 Do you buy things on the internet?
2 Do you look at or write product reviews?

GLOSSARY
product review *(n)* people's opinions and comments about things they buy

B 🔊 **1.45** **LISTEN FOR GIST** **Listen to product reviews from three vloggers. Match the reviews (1, 2, and 3) to the products below.**

an app ___   a TV ___   a tablet ___

C 🔊 **1.45** **LISTEN FOR MAIN IDEAS** **Listen again. How many stars do you think the vloggers give? (Circle) your answer. Then compare with a partner.**

≡ 🛒	≡ 🛒	≡ 🛒
Review one: ★☆☆☆☆ / ★★★★☆	Review two: ★★★☆☆ / ★★★★★	Review three: ★☆☆☆☆ / ★★★☆☆

D **PAIR WORK** **THINK CRITICALLY** **Talk to a partner. Which review is useful to you?**

2 GRAMMAR: *a/an*; adjectives before nouns

A **(Circle) the correct answers. Use the sentences in the grammar box to help you.**

1 Use *a* or *an* with a **singular** / **plural** noun.
2 Use *a* / *an* before most vowel sounds (*a, e, i, o, u*).
3 Use *a* / *an* before a consonant sound (*b, c, d,* …).
4 **Use** / **Don't use** *a* or *an* with plural nouns.

a/an; adjectives before nouns	
a/an	**no** *a/an*
You take **a photo**.	You take **photos**. (plural nouns)
A tablet is expensive.	**This tablet** is expensive. (*this* + noun)
I have **an uncle**.	I have **two uncles**. (number + noun)
We live in **a house**.	**Our house** is small. (possessive adjectives)
You have **a new phone**.	His phone **is new**. (*be* + adjective)

B **Use the words to make sentences. Then check your accuracy.**

1 a / cell phone. / I / new / want _____
2 two / We / in / TVs / our house. / have _____
3 app / really / This / interesting. / is _____
4 you / an / Do / iPad? / have _____
5 like / tablets? / Do / you _____

C ▶ **Now go to page 132. Look at the grammar chart and do the grammar exercise for 4.4.**

✓ **ACCURACY** CHECK

Don't use *a/an* **with a plural noun.**

We have computers at work. ✓
We have ~~a computers~~ at work. ✗

3 PRONUNCIATION: Listening for the end of a sentence

A 🔊 **1.46** **Listen. Which sentence do you hear: A or B? Which speaker is finished?**

1 **A** I love games. ↗
   B I love games. ↘

2 **A** This tablet is great for games. ↗
   B This tablet is great for games. ↘

B 🔊 **1.47** **Listen. Draw one ↗ and one ↘ for each sentence.**

1 I like it because it's small.

2 It's cheap, but it's nice.

3 It's really fast, and it has a nice design.

4 It's expensive because it's a great product.

4 WRITING

A PAIR WORK **Read the product reviews. What are the products? Do you like them? Do you want them?**

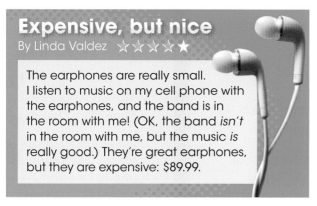

Expensive, but nice
By Linda Valdez ★☆☆☆★

The earphones are really small.
I listen to music on my cell phone with
the earphones, and the band is in
the room with me! (OK, the band *isn't*
in the room with me, but the music *is*
really good.) They're great earphones,
but they are expensive: $89.99.

A cheap chair!
By Carl Rogers ★★☆☆☆

This chair is cheap. It's $29.50.
I have two chairs – one chair
for me, and one chair for my
wife. We sit in them and watch TV. I don't like it
because it's small, and I'm a big man. I don't sit
in the chair. I sit *on* it! Is it comfortable? NO!

GLOSSARY
comfortable (*adj*) good to sit on

B **Read the reviews again. Complete the chart.**

	Earphones	Chair
Title	Expensive, but nice	
Number of stars		
Price ($)		
Good or bad product?		

FIND IT

C **Choose a product you know or find a product on the internet. Find the information in exercise 4B.**

D WRITING SKILLS ⟨Circle⟩ the words *but* and *because* in
the reviews above. Then ⟨circle⟩ the correct answer
in the rules.

1 Use *but* to add an idea that is **the same / different**.

2 Use *because* to **give a reason / ask a question**.

REGISTER CHECK

In informal writing, use exclamation points (!)
after funny sentences or after words and
sentences with a strong feeling, for example,
with *love, like,* or *don't like.*
*I don't sit **in** the chair. I sit **on** it!*
Is it comfortable? NO!

🖊 **WRITE IT**

E **Write reviews for a good product <u>and</u> a bad product.**
Use the products below or your own ideas. Write a title, number of stars, and the price.

| an app | a camera | a desk | a game | a lamp | a tablet | a watch |

F PAIR WORK **Read a partner's reviews. Do you like their products? Do you want them?**

4.5

TIME TO SPEAK
Playlists

A Read the text message. What is the message about?

B 🔊 **1.48** Use words from the message to complete the definitions (1–5). Then listen and check.

1 A playlist is a list of your favorite s_____.
2 People in a b_____ play music or sing.
3 A s_____ is a person in a band. He or she sings the words in a song.
4 F_____ music is music that everyone knows.
5 P_____ music is music that everyone likes.

C **PREPARE** Talk to a partner. Say the name of one singer, one band, and one song you like.

D **DISCUSS** Tell your partner about your favorite music. Make a list of singers, bands, and songs you <u>both</u> like.

E **AGREE** Find singers, bands, and songs that are on your list <u>and</u> on other people's lists. Which music is famous? Which music is popular?

F **DECIDE** Imagine you're going to the party in the text message. Talk to people in your group. Find songs that everyone likes. Then choose <u>ten</u> songs for the party playlist.

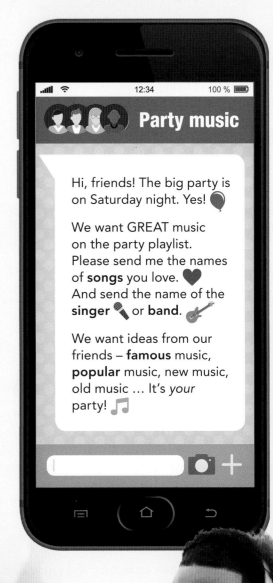

Party music

Hi, friends! The big party is on Saturday night. Yes! 🎈

We want GREAT music on the party playlist. Please send me the names of **songs** you love. ♥ And send the name of the **singer** 🎤 or **band**. 🎸

We want ideas from our friends – **famous** music, **popular** music, new music, old music … It's *your* party! 🎵

> *To check your progress, go to page 153.*

USEFUL PHRASES

 DISCUSS
This song is my favorite.
Me, too!
I don't like this song.

 AGREE
What music do you have on your list?
I have (song/singer/band) on my list.
Let's have this song on the list.
I don't want this song on the list.
What do you think?

✓ **DECIDE**
Do we want (song/singer/band) or (song/singer/band)?
Here are our ten songs for the party playlist.

MONDAYS AND FUN DAYS

5

UNIT OBJECTIVES

- talk about weekday and weekend activities
- tell the time and talk about your routines
- show you agree and have things in common
- write a report about your activities
- compare different work weeks

START SPEAKING

A   **Look at the picture and describe the people. Who are they? Where are they?**

B   **Are they happy? Is it a fun day?**

C   **For you, what is a fun day?**

PLAY OR FAST-FORWARD?

1 VOCABULARY: Days and times of day; everyday activities

A 🔊 **1.49** Listen and repeat. What's your favorite day? What's your favorite time of day?

weekdays					weekend	
Monday	Tuesday	Wednesday	Thursday	Friday	Saturday	Sunday

afternoon

morning

night

evening

Times of day

B 🔊 **1.50** Listen and repeat the sentences.

1 I go out in the evening.

2 I run on Monday and Friday.

3 I work on the weekend.

4 I study in the morning.

5 I don't play soccer.

C **PAIR WORK** Which sentences in exercise 1B are true for you? Tell your partner. Then say <u>two</u> more true sentences about your activities.

D ▶ Now do the vocabulary exercises for 5.1 on page 144.

2 LANGUAGE IN CONTEXT

A Read the article. Who are Sam and Justine? What activities does Sam do on weekdays?

GLOSSARY
after (*adv*) he works, then he plays soccer
before (*adv*) he runs, then he goes to work
every (*det*) 100% (of days / evenings)
way of life (*phrase*) how you live your life

PLAY or FAST-FORWARD?

By Matt Newman

Weekdays = **work** or **study**. **Weekends** = fun. Right? Not for my brother, Sam! For Sam, *every* day is a fun day! He works from **Monday morning** to **Friday afternoon**, but he usually **runs** in the morning before work. On Monday and **Thursday**, he **plays soccer** after work, and he **goes out** with friends on **Wednesday**. He doesn't go out *every* evening – on **Tuesdays** he stays home and watches TV. His way of life is ▶ "play now."

My sister, Justine, is very different. She has fun, but not every day. From Monday to Friday, she works. She doesn't have time for sports, and she hardly ever goes out! It's OK because Justine has free time on the weekend. She chats with family in the afternoon and then goes out with friends at night. Her way of life is work, work, work, and ▶▶ "fast-forward to the weekend."

☺ ☺ Sam and Justine are both happy people, but their ways of life are *very* different. What about you? What's *your* way of life?

B   What's Sam's way of life: "play now", or
    "fast-forward"? What's Justine's way of life?

C   [PAIR WORK] What's your way of life: "play now"
    or "fast-forward to the weekend"? Tell your
    partner. For ideas, watch June's video.

REAL
STUDENT

*Are you the same
as June?*

3   GRAMMAR: Simple present statements with *he, she, they*

A   (Circle) the correct answers. Use the sentences in the grammar box to help you.
    1   In affirmative statements with **he and she** / **they**, most simple present verbs end in -s.
    2   The verb *have* is irregular. In affirmative statements with *he* and *she*, use **have** / **has**.
    3   To make negative statements with *he* and *she*, use **don't** / **doesn't** + verb.

Simple present statements with *he, she, they*

He **works** Monday to Friday.   She **doesn't have** time for sports.

She **chats** with family in the afternoon.   They **don't go out** every evening.

She **has** fun, but not every day.   My dad **doesn't play** soccer.

They **have** fun on the weekend.

B   **Complete the sentences with the words in the box.**

   | doesn't | don't | has | have | play | plays |

    1   My friends _____ video games every weekday evening.
    2   On weekdays, my sister _____ go out in the evening.
    3   Every day, my sister and her husband _____ tea in the morning.
    4   Pedro _____ soccer on his college team, but not in every game.
    5   My mom _____ a tablet, but she doesn't use it.
    6   My grandparents _____ work, so from Monday to Friday
        they're at home.

C   **Look at the sentences in exercise 3B and the adverbs of frequency chart.
    Then (circle) the correct answers.**
    1   My friends *often* / *hardly ever* / *never* play video games.
    2   On weekdays, my sister is *always* / *sometimes* / *never* at home in the evening.
    3   My sister and her husband *always* / *hardly ever* / *never* drink tea in the morning.
    4   Pedro *always* / *sometimes* / *never* plays in his college soccer games.
    5   My mom *always* / *often* / *never* uses her tablet.
    6   My grandparents are *usually* / *hardly ever* / *never* at home on weekdays.

D   ▶   **Now go to page 133. Look at the grammar chart and do the grammar exercise for 5.1.**

Adverbs of frequency

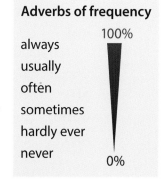

4   SPEAKING

A   **Look at the activities in exercise 1B on page 44. What activities do your family or friends do?
    When do they do them? Write a list. Use adverbs of frequency.**

B   [PAIR WORK] **Talk to a partner about your family and
    friends' activities. Who is "play now"? Who is "fast-forward"?**

    *My sister is "play now." She often
    goes out in the evening ...*

LESSON OBJECTIVE
- tell the time and talk about your routines

1 VOCABULARY: Telling the time

A 🔊 **1.51** [PAIR WORK] **Listen and repeat the times. Then point to a picture and ask** *"What time is it?"* **Your partner says the time.**

It's eight **o'clock**.

It's five-fifteen.
It's **(a) quarter after** five.

It's three-thirty.

It's ten forty-five.
It's **(a) quarter to** eleven.

It's nine-oh-five.
It's five **after** nine.

It's six-fifty.
It's ten **to** seven.

It's **12:00 p.m.** / It's **noon**.
It's **12.00 a.m.** / It's **midnight**.

> ! **a.m.** = before 12 noon
> **p.m.** = after 12 noon
> **to** = before

B ▶ **Now do the first vocabulary exercise for 5.2 on page 145.**

2 LANGUAGE IN CONTEXT

A 🔊 **1.52** **Read and listen. Alex talks to his doctor. What is Alex's problem? What is your "body clock"?**

🔊 **1.52 Audio script**

Alex I'm always so tired.

Doctor Tell me about your routine, Alex. What time do you **get up**?

Alex On weekdays, I usually get up at **7:45**, and I go to class at **8:30**.

Doctor Do you **eat breakfast**?

Alex No, I don't. But I **drink coffee**.

Doctor When do you eat?

Alex At noon. Then I **go to class** again in the afternoon. I usually **have dinner** at **9:00**. My parents don't like that.

Doctor Well, it is very late. Do they have dinner before you?

Alex Yes, they do. Usually at **6:00**.

Doctor Does your mom make dinner for you?

Alex No, she doesn't. I make it.

Doctor OK. What do you do on weekends?

Alex On Friday and Saturday, I go out with friends. I usually **go to bed** at **2:00** or **3:00** a.m. And on Sunday, I get up really late and watch TV.

Doctor Alex, it's time to listen to your body clock!

B 🔊 **1.52** [PAIR WORK] **Listen again. Write notes about Alex's routine. Compare with a partner.**

He doesn't eat breakfast. He drinks coffee.

C ▶ **Now do the second vocabulary exercise for 5.2 on page 145.**

D [PAIR WORK] **Is your routine the same as or different from Alex's? Tell your partner. For ideas, watch Josue's video.**

REAL STUDENT

Is your routine different from Josue's, or the same?

3 GRAMMAR: Questions in the simple present

A **Circle** the correct answers. Use the sentences in the grammar box to help you.

1 With the pronouns *I, you, we,* and *they,* use **Do / Does**.

2 With the pronouns *he, she,* and *it,* use **Do / Does**.

3 In yes/no questions, the word order is **Do or Does + person or thing + verb / Do or Does + verb + person or thing**.

4 In information questions, put the question word(s) (for example, *Where* or *What time*) **before / after** *do* and *does.*

Questions in the simple present

Yes/no **questions**

Do I **have** class today?

Do you **go out** with friends?

Does he **go** to classes every day?

Does it **have** good apps?

Do they **have** dinner before you?

Information questions

How do I **get** to class?

What time do you **go out** with friends?

When does he **go** to classes?

What does it **have**?

Where do they **eat** dinner?

B PAIR WORK Complete the conversations. Use the audio script on page 46 to help you. Then practice them with a partner.

1 A _____ _____ do you go to work?

   B I _____ to work at 7:00.

   A Wow! _____ do you go to bed?

   B I usually go to bed after midnight. I'm always tired!

2 A _____ they play soccer?

   B _____, they do. What about you?

   A No, I _____ .

3 A _____ Martin have a new job?

   B Yes, he _____ .

   A _____ does he work?

   B He _____ in an office.

C ▶ **Now go to page 133. Look at the grammar charts and do the grammar exercise for 5.2.**

D Write <u>three</u> questions about your partner's routine. Use the words in the box to start your questions. Then check your accuracy.

> Do … ?   What … ?   What time … ?
> When … ?   Where … ?

✓ **ACCURACY** CHECK

Use *do* or *does* with information questions in the simple present.

Where Margaret work? ✗
Where does Margaret work? ✓

E PAIR WORK **Ask and answer the questions from exercise 3D with a partner.**

4 SPEAKING

A **Think about your routines and your family's routines. What do you do? When do you do it?**

B PAIR WORK **Ask your partner about their routines and their family's routines. Do they listen to their body clock?**

> When do you get up?

> I usually get up at 7:30, but my sister gets up at 5:00!

5.3 ME, TOO

LESSON OBJECTIVE
- show you agree and have things in common

1 FUNCTIONAL LANGUAGE

A 🔊 **1.53** **The men are at work. Read and listen to their conversation. What do both the men do?**

🔊 **1.53 Audio script**

A Do you always run at lunchtime?

B Yeah, I usually run for about 30 minutes.

A That's cool. It's good to go out.

B **I agree.** And what about you? Do you run?

A Hardly ever. Well, I play basketball.

B So you run a lot!

A **That's true.** But I don't have the ball a lot! I'm not very good.

B **Me, neither.** But basketball is fun.

A **Yeah, I know.**

B I play with friends.

A **Me, too.** Hey, we have a game on Thursday after work. Play with us!

B Thursday. Um … yeah, OK.

A Great! Now I'm not the only bad player.

B Very funny!

B **Complete the chart with expressions in bold from the conversations above.**

Showing you agree	Showing you have things in common
I ¹ _____ . That's ² _____ . / That's right. ³ _____ , I know.	⁴ _____ , neither. (-) Me, ⁵ _____ . (+)

C **Choose the correct answers to complete the conversations. Then practice with a partner.**

1 A I play basketball on the weekend.

   B *Me, too / Me, neither.* I play on Sunday.

2 A Soccer is great.

   B I *agree / right.* Do you play?

3 A This game is boring.

   B *Yeah, I know / Me, neither.* The team isn't very good.

4 A I don't get up late on Saturday.

   B *Me, too / Me, neither.* I get up at 8.

2 REAL-WORLD STRATEGY

SHORT ANSWERS WITH ADVERBS OF FREQUENCY
People sometimes answer questions with adverbs of frequency, not complete sentences.
A Do you always run at lunch?
B Usually. And what about you? Do you run?
A Hardly ever.

A   **Read about short answers with adverbs of frequency in the box above. Who runs a lot: A or B? Who doesn't run a lot?**

B   🔊 **1.54 Listen to a conversation. Who gets up early on the weekend: the man, the woman, or both of them?**

C   🔊 **1.55 Listen again. What one-word answer does the man say? What one-word answer does the woman say?**

D   ▶ **PAIR WORK** **Student A: Go to page 157. Student B: Go to page 159. Follow the instructions.**

3 PRONUNCIATION: Saying syllables in words

A   🔊 **1.55 Listen. How many syllables do you hear? Write 1, 2, or 3.**

   1 run __   **2** basketball __   **3** soccer __

B   🔊 **1.56 Say the words. How many syllables are there? Write 1, 2, or 3. Listen and check.**

   1 weekend __   **3** usually __   **5** sport __
   2 Wednesday __   **4** chat __   **6** morning __

C   **Look at the audio script on page 48. Find more examples of words with one or two syllables.**

4 SPEAKING

A   **Write a list of things you do often. Write how you feel about the activities.**

   chat with friends online – fun

   watch TV – interesting

B   **PAIR WORK** **Tell your partner what you do and how you feel about the activities. Your partner says when he/she agrees and when you have things in common. Then change roles and repeat.**

> On weekdays, I watch TV in the evening.

> Me, too.

> It's sometimes interesting.

> Yeah, I know.

A HAPPY LIFE

1 READING

A **SKIM** Look at the picture and the title. What is the magazine article about?

WORK, REST, and PLAY = The **WRAP** test

Doctors always say, for a happy life, work, rest, and play! OK, but it isn't always easy. What about *your* life? Do you work, rest, and play? Do you work, rest, and play? Or do you work, rest, and play?

Look at Cheryl.

She's very busy. She's a salesperson. She works at a store Monday to Friday from 10:00 a.m. to 5:30 p.m. She has a French class in the evening on Tuesdays and Thursdays. After class, she listens to music or watches TV. Then she does her homework. On the weekend, she has free time. She plays soccer with her friends. She often goes out with her sister on Saturday night. On Sunday, she studies French for her class. Then she sometimes plays the guitar.

What is Cheryl's WRAP?
What about you? To find out, take the WRAP test …

B **READ FOR DETAILS** Read the article again. Complete the chart with the correct verbs.

Work		Rest		Play	
works	at a store		music		soccer
	a French class		TV		with her sister
	her homework				the guitar
	French				

C **PAIR WORK** **THINK CRITICALLY** Which WRAP result is true for Cheryl?

1 **work**, **rest**, and play   2 **work**, rest, and **play**   3 work, **rest**, and **play**

2 WRITING

A **Read Andre's WRAP report. What does he do on weekdays? What does he do on the weekend?**

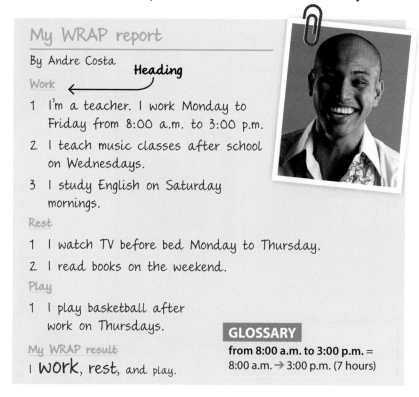

My WRAP report

By Andre Costa

Heading

Work ←

1 I'm a teacher. I work Monday to Friday from 8:00 a.m. to 3:00 p.m.

2 I teach music classes after school on Wednesdays.

3 I study English on Saturday mornings.

Rest

1 I watch TV before bed Monday to Thursday.

2 I read books on the weekend.

Play

1 I play basketball after work on Thursdays.

My WRAP result

I **work, rest,** and play.

REGISTER CHECK

Write *a.m.* and *p.m.* after times.
I work Monday to Friday from 8:00 a.m. to 3:00 p.m.

Say *in the morning, in the afternoon,* or *at night* after times.
Andre says, "I sometimes go to bed at 1:30 in the morning."

GLOSSARY

from 8:00 a.m. to 3:00 p.m. =
8:00 a.m. → 3:00 p.m. (7 hours)

B **WRITING SKILLS** **Look at the heading "Work." Circle the other headings in the report. What do they show?**

a days and times in the report

b different sports in each part of the report

c the different topics in the report

C **Look at the numbered lists in the report above. What do the lists show?**

a Andre's test results (= answers)

b Andre's activities

c Andre's classes

D **Write notes in the chart below with your information. Use the chart in exercise 1B for an example.**

Work	Rest	Play

WRITE IT

E **Write your WRAP report. Use headings and numbered lists. Include activities, times, and days.**

F **PAIR WORK** **Work with a partner. Read your partner's report. What's his/her WRAP result?**

G **GROUP WORK** **Compare reports in your group. Tell the group about your partner.**

Sora works at a restaurant on the weekend. She ...

TIME TO SPEAK
Life = 5 + 2

A **PREPARE** Read the magazine article about different work weeks. Which week is your favorite: A, B, or C? Tell your partner.

END OF THE
TWO-DAY WEEKEND?

For a lot of people, life = 5 + 2. They work 5 days and have 2 days for the weekend. But is this good? Imagine:

Week A	We work 4 long days (10 hours) and have 3 days for the weekend.
Week B	We work 6 short days (6½ hours) and have 1 day for the weekend.
Week C	We work 7 very short days (5½ hours) and don't have a weekend.

B **DISCUSS** Imagine you have a "week A" life. Talk to a partner. Describe your routine. What do you do, and when do you do it? Then talk about week B and week C.

C **DECIDE** Which week is good for your body clock: A, B, C, or "5 + 2"? Why?

D **AGREE** Tell the class which week is your favorite. Which week does everyone like? Which week does no one like?

》》 To check your progress, go to page 153. 》》

USEFUL PHRASES

 PREPARE
Which week is your favorite?
Week … is my favorite.

 DISCUSS
I have a week A/B/C life.
I get up / have breakfast at …
I work from … to …
Before/After work, I …
I have free time from … to …

 DECIDE
Week … is good for me because …
I like / don't like week … because …
I want free time on the weekends / in the evenings.
I like long /short work days.

UNIT OBJECTIVES

- talk about places in the city
- talk about nature in your area
- ask for and give directions
- write a fact sheet about a place in nature
- plan a new neighborhood for a city

ZOOM IN, ZOOM OUT

6

START SPEAKING

A **Say things you see in the picture. For ideas, watch Julieth's video.**

B **Do you want to go here? Why or why not?**

C **Do you like cities? Do you like places in nature? Which is your favorite?**

REAL STUDENT

Do you see the same things as Julieth?

GOOD PLACES

1 LANGUAGE IN CONTEXT

A 🔊 **1.57** **Lucas and Robert are in New York City. Read and listen to their conversation. Where is Lucas from? Where is Robert from? What does Lucas want to do on Saturday?**

B 🔊 **1.57** **Read and listen again. Are the sentences true or false?**

1 Lucas has a lot of time in New York City.

2 There is no restaurant in the hotel.

GLOSSARY
neighborhood (*n*) an area of a city

🔊 **1.57 Audio script**

Lucas I'm here, in New York City, for a week. And then I go home to Paris on Sunday.

Robert So you don't have a lot of time to see my great city.

Lucas No, I don't. There's no free time this week – it's work, work, work! But I have some time on Saturday.

Robert OK. There are a lot of places to see and things to do on the weekend. Where is your **hotel**?

Lucas It's near Central Park.

Robert No way! Central Park is great. There are some interesting museums near the **park**. Oh, and there's a **zoo** in the park!

Lucas Cool! What about places to eat? There's no **restaurant** in my hotel.

Robert Hmm … for breakfast, there's a nice **café** near here. And there are a lot of great restaurants in this neighborhood, too.

Lucas Great. Do you know some good **stores**? I don't have a lot of free time, but …

Robert Oh, yeah. There are a lot of great stores in New York. So … no museum, no park, no zoo – just shopping?

Lucas Yes!

INSIDER ENGLISH

Use *No way!* to show surprise.
No way! Central Park is great.

2 VOCABULARY: Places in cities

A 🔊 **1.58** **Listen and repeat the words.**

bookstore

hospital

movie theater

restaurant

supermarket

café

hotel

museum

school

zoo

college

mall

park

store

B ▶ **Now do the vocabulary exercises for 6.1 on page 145.**

C `PAIR WORK` **Which three places in cities do you both like? Which three <u>don't</u> you like?**

3 GRAMMAR: *There's, There are; a lot of, some, no*

A ⟨Circle⟩ **the correct answers. Use the sentences in the grammar box to help you.**

1 Use *There's* with **singular** / **plural** nouns.

2 Use *There are* with **singular** / **plural** nouns.

3 Use *an* / *no* in negative sentences.

4 Use *some* **for exact numbers** / **when you don't know how many things there are**.

There's (= There is), There are; a lot of, some, no

There's no free time this week.

There's a zoo in the park.

There's a nice café near here.

There are some interesting museums near the park.

There are a lot of good places to see on the weekend.

no = zero

a/an = one

some = a small number

a lot of = a large number

B ⟨Circle⟩ **the correct words to complete the sentences.**

1 *There's / There are* a lot of stores in the mall.

2 *There's / There are* a supermarket near the college.

3 There are *a / some* good cafés on Boston Road.

4 There's *a / a lot of* big hospital in the city.

5 There are *a lot of / no* stores, so it's great for shopping.

6 In my city, there are *a / no* zoos.

C ▶ **Now go to page 134. Look at the grammar chart and do the grammar exercise for 6.1.**

D **Write sentences about your city. Use** *there is/there are, a/an, some, a lot of,* **and** *no.* **Then check your accuracy.**

There's _____ .

There's _____ .

There are _____ .

There are _____ .

There is/are no _____ .

✓ **ACCURACY** CHECK

Use *there are*, <u>not</u> *there is*, before *a lot of* and *some* + plural noun.

There ~~is~~ some museums in this city. ✗

There are some museums in this city. ✓

E PAIR WORK **Compare your sentences with a partner.**

4 SPEAKING

PAIR WORK **Talk about the things in your neighborhood. Then compare with a partner. What's the same? What's different?**

There are some good restaurants near my home.

Same! And there's a movie theater near my home.

CITY LIFE, WILD LIFE

1 VOCABULARY: Nature

A 🔊 **1.59** **Listen and repeat the words. Which picture is your favorite? Which words describe water?**

  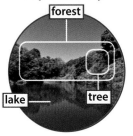 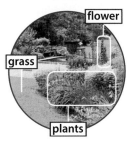 

snow mountains island forest flower hill
river beach lake tree grass desert
ocean plants

B **Cross out the word that does not belong.**

1	lake	~~flower~~	ocean	**3**	river	desert	lake
2	plants	trees	snow	**4**	grass	beach	ocean

5	forest	ocean	trees
6	mountain	hill	island

C ▶ **Now do the vocabulary exercises for 6.2 on page 146.**

2 LANGUAGE IN CONTEXT

A **Read the article. Choose a good title.**

1 What's your favorite city?   2 Are you close to nature?   3 Do you like nature?

B [PAIR WORK] **Take the test. Then compare your answers with a partner.**

Do I like nature? Sure. We all love flowers and trees. But I live in a big city, so I don't live close to nature … Or do I? What about you? Take the test. For each sentence, circle all the answers that are true for you.

	In your neighborhood	In your city (e.g., in a park)	1–3 hours from your city	Not near your city
There's a lot of **grass**.	A	B	C	D
There are a lot of **flowers**.	A	B	C	D
There are some **trees**.	A	B	C	D
There's a **river**.	A	B	C	D
There's a **lake**.	A	B	C	D
There's a **forest**.	A	B	C	D
There are some **mountains and hills**.	A	B	C	D
There's a **beach**.	A	B	C	D
There's an **ocean**.	A	B	C	D
There are a lot of **plants**.	A	B	C	D

♡ 21   💬 25   💭 14   **A** = 3 points,   **B** = 2 points,   **C** = 1 point,   **D** = 0 points

Are you close to nature?
45–60 points
Nature is everywhere!
30–44 points
There's a lot of nature near you.
15–29 points
There's some nature near you.
1–14 points
There isn't a lot of nature near you.
0 points
You only see nature on TV!

C [PAIR WORK] **Give examples of nature in your city. For ideas, watch Larissa's video.**

 **REAL STUDENT**

Are your answers the same as Larissa's?

3 GRAMMAR: Count and non-count nouns

A (Circle) the correct answers. Use the sentences in the grammar box to help you.

1 Count nouns have **plural and singular forms / no singular or plural form**.

2 Use *a/an* with **singular / plural** count nouns.

3 Use *There's / There are* with plural count nouns.

4 Use *There's / There are* with singular count nouns and non-count nouns.

Count and non-count nouns		
Singular	**Plural**	**No singular or plural form**
There's a **river** in my city.	There are two **rivers**.	There's no / some / a lot of **grass**.
There's an **ocean** near here.	There are no **oceans** near here.	There's no / some / a lot of **water** in the ocean.
	There are some **plants**.	
	There are a lot of **flowers**.	

B Complete the sentences with the correct form of the nouns in parentheses ( ).

1 There are no _____*trees*_____ (tree) in my neighborhood.

2 There's an _____ (ocean) three hours from my city.

3 There's a lot of _____ (nature) in this city.

4 There are some _____ (restaurant) on my street.

5 There is no _____ (grass) near my house.

6 There are a lot of _____ (hotel) in my city.

C ▶ **Now go to page 134. Look at the grammar chart and do the grammar exercise for 6.2.**

D PAIR WORK Change the sentences in exercise 3B so they're true for you and your city. Compare your sentences with a partner.

> There are some trees in my neighborhood.

4 SPEAKING

A Choose a city in your country or in a different country. Think about the nature there.

B PAIR WORK Work with a partner. Tell your partner about the place. Does your partner know the place?

> There's a beach in the city.
> There are no hills or mountains.
> There are a lot of trees ...

> I know! It's Tampa, in the U.S.!

IS IT NEAR HERE?

City Museum, Garcia Moreno

Garcia Moreno

🏛 City Museum

1 FUNCTIONAL LANGUAGE

A **Look at the pictures. The woman is in Quito, Ecuador. What places do you see on the map on her phone?**

B 🔊 **1.60** **Read and listen. The woman asks two people for directions. What places does she ask about?**

🔊 **1.60 Audio script**

1 A Excuse me. Do you speak English?

B Yes, I do.

A Oh, good! **Where's** Garcia Moreno Street? **Is it near here?**

B Yes, it is. Uh … turn left here. **Go one block**, and then **turn right**. **That's** Garcia Moreno Street.

A OK, great! Thanks.

2 A Excuse me. **Is this** Garcia Moreno Street?

B Yes, it is.

A Where's the City Museum?

B **It's that way. Go straight. It's on the left.** Or come with me! It's on my way to the supermarket.

C **Complete the chart with expressions in bold from the conversations above.**

Asking for directions	Giving directions
Where am I? / Where are we?	Turn left. / 4 _____.
I don't understand the map.	5 _____ way.
1 _____ Garcia Moreno Street?	Go one 6 _____. / Go 7 _____.
Is it 2 _____ ?	It's on the right. / 8 _____.
Excuse me. Is 3 _____ Garcia Moreno Street?	It's over there. / It's here!
	9 _____ Garcia Moreno Street.
	Look on your phone. Zoom in / zoom out. It's here.

D 🔊 **1.61** PAIR WORK **Complete the conversations. Then listen and check. Practice with a partner.**

1 A Excuse me. *It's / Where's* Central Station?

B Go one *way / block*. It's on the left.

2 A *Is this / Is it* San Gabriel Street?

B No. *Turn / It's* right. That's San Gabriel Street.

3 A Is the language center *go straight / near here*?

B Yes. It's over *there / go one block*.

2 REAL-WORLD STRATEGY

A 🔊 **1.62** **Listen to a conversation. Where does the man want to go?**

B 🔊 **1.62** **Listen again. The man wants to check the information. What does he do?**

    1 He asks the woman to repeat her words.   **2** He repeats the woman's words.

> **CHECKING INFORMATION**
>
> To check you understand, say *So, …* and repeat the information.
> *It's that way. Turn left here. Go one block, and then turn right.*
> *So, turn left here. Go one block, and then turn right.*

C 🔊 **1.63** **Read about checking information in the box above. Then listen to the directions. Check the information.**

    1 Turn right here. Then turn right again.   *So, turn right here. Then turn right again.*

D ▶ PAIR WORK **Student A: Go to page 157. Student B: Go to page 159. Follow the instructions.**

3 PRONUNCIATION: Saying /ɪr/ and /er/ sounds

A 🔊 **1.64** **Listen and repeat. Focus on the sound of the letters in bold.**

    /ɪr/ Is it n**ear here**?   /er/ Wh**ere** is th**eir** house?

B 🔊 **1.65** **Listen. Write A for words with /ɪr/. Write B for words with /er/.**

1 clear ___	**3** chair ___	**5** there ___	**7** year ___
2 they're ___	**4** earphones ___	**6** parent ___	**8** square ___

C 🔊 **1.66** PAIR WORK **Listen to the conversations. Then practice with a partner.**

    1 **A** Wh**ere**'s Bl**air** Street?

        B It's n**ear here**. Go to the town sq**uare** and then turn right.

    2 **A** Wh**ere** are your p**a**rents?

        B Th**ey're** over th**ere**, on the ch**airs**.

4 SPEAKING

A PAIR WORK **Put the conversation in order. Then practice it with a partner.**

    ___ So, go straight. Then turn left. It's on the left.

    ___ Yes.

    ___ Excuse me. Where's the Park Hotel?

    ___ It's that way. Go straight. Then turn left. It's on the left.

B **Work alone. Choose <u>one</u> of the situations below.**

    1 Imagine you are at the City Museum in Quito, Ecuador. Look at the map on the cell phone on page 58. Choose a place to go.

    2 Imagine you are in another city. You can go online and find a map of the city. Choose where you are and a place to go.

FIND IT

C PAIR WORK **Ask a partner for directions. You can use your phone to help you. Then change roles.**

6.4 A FOREST IN THE CITY

LESSON OBJECTIVE
■ write a fact sheet about a place in nature

1 LISTENING

A Look at the pictures. Where is the woman? What do you see?

B ◁)) **1.67** **LISTEN FOR DETAILS** Listen to the podcast *Walk with Yasmin*. Where is the forest?

C ◁)) **1.67** **LISTEN FOR EXAMPLES** Listen again. Check (✓) the words Yasmin says.

Forest
- ☐ animals
- ☐ flowers
- ☐ grass
- ☐ a mountain
- ☐ an ocean
- ☐ plants
- ☐ a river
- ☐ trees

City
- ☐ hospitals
- ☐ hotels
- ☐ museums
- ☐ people
- ☐ restaurants
- ☐ schools
- ☐ stores
- ☐ zoos

2 PRONUNCIATION: Listening for important words

A ◁)) **1.68** Read the sentences below. Focus on the <u>underlined</u> words. Then listen. Which sentence do you hear, A or B?

A There <u>are</u> some tall trees <u>and</u> a lot <u>of</u> big plants here.

B There are some <u>tall trees</u> and a <u>lot</u> of <u>big plants</u> here.

B ◁)) **1.69** <u>Underline</u> the important words in each sentence. Listen and check.

1 There's a river near me. (1 word)

2 There are a lot of interesting animals here. (3 words)

3 I'm on a mountain in a forest. (2 words)

4 There's an ocean and some beautiful beaches. (3 words)

A **Read the fact sheet. What is in Tijuca Forest?**

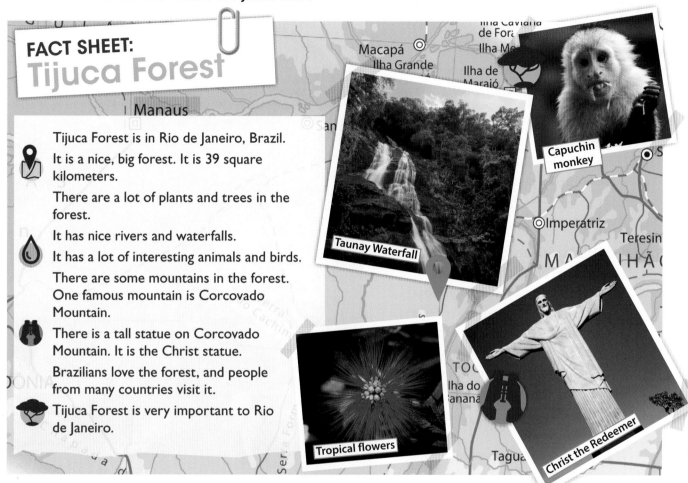

FACT SHEET:
Tijuca Forest

Tijuca Forest is in Rio de Janeiro, Brazil.

It is a nice, big forest. It is 39 square kilometers.

There are a lot of plants and trees in the forest.

It has nice rivers and waterfalls.

It has a lot of interesting animals and birds.

There are some mountains in the forest. One famous mountain is Corcovado Mountain.

There is a tall statue on Corcovado Mountain. It is the Christ statue.

Brazilians love the forest, and people from many countries visit it.

Tijuca Forest is very important to Rio de Janeiro.

Capuchin monkey

Taunay Waterfall

Tropical flowers

Christ the Redeemer

B **PAIR WORK** **THINK CRITICALLY** **There are <u>no</u> contractions in the fact sheet (for example, *It's, There's*). Why not?**

C **Read the sentences from the fact sheet. <u>Underline</u> two opinion adjectives and one size adjective.**

It has a lot of interesting animals and birds.

It is a nice, big forest.

D **WRITING SKILLS** **Read the rules below. (Circle) *before* or *after*. Use the sentences in exercise 3C to help you.**

1 *Some, a lot of,* and *no* go **before** / **after** opinion adjectives (for example, *good, nice, interesting*).

2 Opinion adjectives usually go **before** / **after** size adjectives (for example, *big, small, tall*).

REGISTER CHECK

Really and *very* make adjectives stronger. Use *very* in writing. *Really* is common in speaking.

*Tijuca Forest is **very** important to Rio de Janeiro.*

E **Choose a natural area to write about. You can go online to find facts about where it is, how big it is, what nature is there, and who goes to it. Use *very*. Do <u>not</u> use contractions. Remember to write adjectives in the correct order.**

FIND IT

F **Write a fact sheet about a place in nature. Write five or six sentences. Use the fact sheet in exercise 3A for an example.**

6.5

TIME TO SPEAK
A good place to live

A **PREPARE** Talk to a partner. What do you see in the pictures?

B **DISCUSS** Which places in the pictures are important to have near your home? Write numbers 1–8 next to the pictures.

1 = very important → 8 = not very important

C **DISCUSS** Imagine that city planners want ideas for a new neighborhood in your city. Work with a partner. Choose <u>one</u> person from the list below. What does your person want in the new neighborhood? Write notes.

- You have young children.
- You are over 60 and you don't work.
- You are a young person in your first apartment.
- You are a college student in a home-share.

D **PRESENT** Present your ideas for the new neighborhood to the class. Which things does everyone think are important in a city?

>> *To check your progress, go to page 153.*

USEFUL PHRASES

DISCUSS
I have children. A school is really important.
What about … ? Me, too. I agree. / I disagree.
I think … is good for the neighborhood.
I want … for the neighborhood.

I like / don't like …
I think … are very important / not very important.

PRESENT
We want …
Everyone in the class likes …

62

REVIEW 2 (UNITS 4–6)

1 VOCABULARY

A Look at the groups of words in 1–6. In each group, (circle) the word that does not belong. Then match the groups with the categories (a–f).

1	grass	mountain	river	song	tree	___	**a** technology
2	call friends	get up	hill	play soccer	work	___	**b** music
3	album	band	camera	playlist	singer	___	**c** places in cities
4	afternoon	hotel	Monday	morning	night	___	**d** nature
5	app	laptop	morning	phone	tablet	___	**e** things we do
6	café	hospital	restaurant	run	store	___	**f** days and times of day

B Match each word you (circled) in 1–6 to a different category (a–f). Then add <u>one</u> extra word to the categories.

2 GRAMMAR

A Make questions and answers. Use the words in parentheses ( ) and *do/does/don't/doesn't*.

1 A _____ you _____ video games?

B Yes, I sometimes _____ games on my cell phone. (play)

2 A Where _____ you _____ at lunchtime?

B I usually _____ at home. (eat)

3 A _____ your grandfather _____?

B Yes, he _____ at the hospital. (work)

4 A _____ you and your family _____ soccer?

B No, we _____ it. (like)

5 A What _____ your parents _____ on TV?

B Not a lot! They _____ usually _____ TV. (watch)

6 A _____ your children _____ phones?

B My daughter has a cell phone, but my son _____ one. (have)

B PAIR WORK Ask and answer <u>five</u> questions about things you and your family do.

C (Circle) the correct answers.

I ¹ *work / works* in a hotel. It's an expensive hotel with ² *a / some* really nice rooms. It's next to a big park. ³ *There's / There are* a lot of trees, and ⁴ *there's / there are* a lake, too. It's really nice in the park, so I ⁵ *often / never* go at lunchtime, and I ⁶ *have / has* lunch near the lake.

D Write a description of a nice place. Write how often you go there.

3 SPEAKING

A PAIR WORK Talk about a place. Describe it or say what you do there. Your partner guesses the place. Then change roles.

> There's a couch, and there are some chairs. I often watch TV in the evening.

> It's your living room.

B Write three sentences to describe a place from exercise 3A. Then compare with a partner.

4 FUNCTIONAL LANGUAGE

A (Circle) **the correct answers.**

Felix   Your photos are great.

Maya   Thanks. My phone has a good camera.

Felix   ¹ *See / So*, all the pictures are from the camera on your cell phone.

Maya   Yes, that's ² *fine / right*. I always use my cell phone camera.

Felix   ³ *Hey. / Yeah*.

Maya   ⁴ *What / Where* about you?

Felix   I always use my phone, too. I don't have a different camera.

Maya   ⁵ *Me, / My* neither. I don't want a different camera. They're really big …

Felix   Yeah, I ⁶ *know / do*. And they're expensive.

Maya   ⁷ *That's / There's* true.

B **Complete the conversation with the words in the box. There are <u>two</u> extra words.**

turn	way	to	me	you	near

A Excuse ¹_____ . Where's the zoo?

B The zoo?

A Yes. Is it ²_____ here?

B Yes. It's that ³_____ . Go one block, and then ⁴_____ left.

5 SPEAKING

A | PAIR WORK | **Choose <u>one</u> of the conversations below. Ask and answer the questions with a partner.**

1 What technology do you have? How often do you use it?

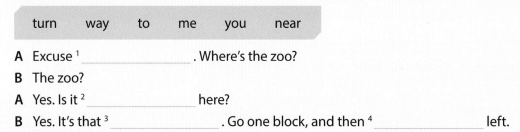

> I have a laptop, a phone, and a TV. I use my laptop every day. I send emails, and I …

2 What do you on weekdays? When do you do fun things?

> On weekdays, I go to work. I get up at 7:00 a.m., and then I …

3 What's a good place to go to in or near your city? Where is it?

> There's a new Chinese restaurant near here. It's really good.

> Yeah. Where is it?

B | PAIR WORK | **Change roles and repeat the conversation.**

GRAMMAR REFERENCE AND PRACTICE

1.1 *I AM, YOU ARE* (page 3)

I am (= I'm), you are (= you're)				
	Affirmative (+)	**Negative (-)**	**Question**	**Short answers**
I	**I'm** from Lima.	**I'm not** from Mexico City.	**Am I** in room 6B?	Yes, **you are.** / No, **you're not.**
You	**You're** from Paris.	**You're not** from Bogotá.	**Are you** from Tokyo?	Yes, **I am.** / No, **I'm not.**

A Match 1–6 to a–f to make sentences.

1 I'm	**a** not.	**4** Are you	**d** am.
2 I'm from	**b** Mexican.	**5** Yes, I	**e** Brazil?
3 No, I'm	**c** Honduras.	**6** Are you from	**f** Chinese?

1.2 *WHAT'S … ?, IT'S …* (page 5)

What's … ? (= What is)	*It's … (= It is)*
What's your first name?	**It's** Juana.
What's the name of your college?	**It's** Garcia College.
What's your email address?	**It's** juanagarcia@bestmail.com.

> **!** Don't repeat the subject of the question:
> ~~The name of my company is~~
> It's Dallas Sales.

A Put the words in order to make sentences.

1 first / is / My / Ruby. / name

2 is / address / My / dfox@kmail.com. / email

3 Green College. / my college / of / The name / is

4 my company / Dallas Sales. / The name / is / of

2.1 *IS / ARE* IN STATEMENTS AND *YES/NO* QUESTIONS (page 13)

is / are in statements and *yes/no* questions			
	Affirmative	**Question**	**Short answers**
He / She / It	**'s** ten. (*'s = is*)	**Is** he your husband? **Is** she your friend?	Yes, he **is.** / No, he**'s not.** Yes, she **is.** / No, she**'s not.**
You / We / They	**'re** cousins. (*'re = are*)	**Are** you brothers? **Are** they your children?	Yes, we **are.** / No, we**'re not.** Yes, they **are.** / No, they**'re not.**

A Write sentences and questions with *is* and *are*.

1 she / 22   *She's 22.*

2 they / your cousins   ?

3 he / 18   ?

4 my grandparents / Brazilian   .

5 we / in Room 5B   ?

6 no, you / not   .

2.2 IS NOT / ARE NOT (page 15)

is not (= 's not) / are not (= 're not)	
He / She / It	**'s not** in Rio de Janeiro.
You / We / They	**'re not** shy.

isn't (= is not) / aren't (= are not)		
Jack	**isn't**	boring.
The students	**aren't**	in the class room.

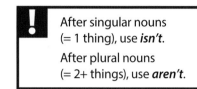

After singular nouns
(= 1 thing), use **isn't**.
After plural nouns
(= 2+ things), use **aren't**.

A (Circle) the correct words to complete the sentences.

1 Jan *is / isn't* from New York City.
   He's from Miami.

2 *She's / She's not* 18. She's not 20.

3 Daniel is in Moscow. *He's / He's not* in
   St. Petersburg.

4 You're not shy. *You're / You're not* really friendly!

5 My cousins are in Japan. *They're / They're not* in
   the U.S.

6 *We're / We're not* sisters. We're friends.

3.1 POSSESSIVE ADJECTIVES; POSSESSIVE *'S* AND *S'* (page 23)

Possessive adjectives	
I → **my**	This is **my** apartment.
he → **his**	**His** name is Sergei.
she → **her**	It's **her** favorite picture.w
it → **its**	Nice cat! What's **its** name?
you → **your**	Is this **your** room?
we → **our**	**Our** home is in La Paz.
they → **their**	Rita is **their** daughter.

Possessive *'s* and *s'*
Add possessive *'s* to a singular noun. (= 1 thing)
This is Sergei**'s** room.
My mother**'s** name is Kate.
Add possessive *'* after the *s* of a plural noun. (= 2+ things)
This is his parent**s'** house.
My cousin**s'** house is in Rio.

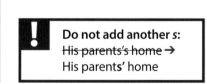

Do not add another *s*:
His parents's home →
His parents' home

A (Circle) the correct words to complete the sentences.

1 *My / I* email address is sky121@bestmail.com.

2 My *friends / friend's* name is Ramona.

3 This is *his / he's* hotel room.

4 Excuse me. What's *you / your* name?

5 This is my *parents's / parents'* new car.

6 David is *our / we* son.

7 The name of *Ann's / Anns'* company is Mason Sales.

8 What's *they're / their* telephone number?

3.2 *IT IS* (page 25)

> **!** *It* is a pronoun. *It* is always singular. Use *it* for things. For example, *the house = it*. Use *isn't* after nouns. Use *'s not* after pronouns.

It is in statements and *yes/no* questions

	Affirmative	Negative	Question	Short answers
The house	**is** small.	**isn't** small. (*isn't = is not*)	**Is it** small?	Yes, **it is.**
It's (= *it is*)	small.	**not** small.		No, **it's not.**

A Answer the questions so they're true for you. Write statements. Use *It's* and *It's not* to give more information.

1 Is your home an apartment?   *My home isn't an apartment. It's a house.*

2 Is your bedroom cool?

3 Is your kitchen big?

4 Is your parents' house old?

5 Is your friend's TV new?

6 Is your refrigerator tall?

3.4 INFORMATION QUESTIONS WITH *BE* (page 28)

Question word		*be*	
What		**is**	your name?
Where		**is**	the house?
How old		**are**	they?
Who		**are**	they?
How many	people	**are**	in the house?
How many	rooms	**are**	in it?

> **!** Information questions ask for information about, for example, people, places, age, time, and quantity. Don't answer information questions with *yes/no* answers.
>
> Use *is* to talk about 1 thing. Use *are* to talk about 2+ things. Use a noun after *How many … ?*

A Put the words in the correct order to make questions.

1 is / Who / brother? / your   *Who is your brother?*

2 you? / How / are / old

3 her / is / college? / Where

4 email / is / What / address? / your

5 many / are / people / How / the house? / in

6 apartment? / is / his / Where

4.1 SIMPLE PRESENT STATEMENTS WITH *I, YOU, WE* (page 35)

Simple present statements with *I, you, we*

	Affirmative	Negative
I / You / We	**have** a smartwatch.	**don't have** a smartwatch.
	like my phone.	**don't like** my phone.
	love games.	**don't love** games.
	want a tablet.	**don't want** a tablet.

A **Put the words in order to make sentences.**

1 games. / like / I _____

2 your / I / smartwatch. / love _____

3 don't / I / a / laptop. / have _____

4 a / tablet. / want / We _____

5 like / don't / laptops. / You _____

6 camera. / want / I / don't / a _____

4.2 SIMPLE PRESENT *YES/NO* QUESTIONS WITH *I, YOU, WE* (page 37)

Simple present *yes/no* questions with *I, you, we*	
yes/no questions	Short answers
Do I **send** nice emails?	Yes, you **do.** / No, you **don't.**
Do we **post** good photos?	Yes, you **do.** / No, you **don't.**
Do you **use** social media?	Yes, I **do.** / No, I **don't.**
Do you **and your friends play** games?	Yes, we **do.** / No, we **don't.**

A **Write questions. Then answer the questions so they're true for you.**

1 you / call your family / on the weekends   <u>Do you call your family on the weekends</u> ? <u>Yes, I do</u> .

2 you / post comments / on Twitter   _____ ? _____ .

3 you / send text messages / to your parents   _____ ? _____ .

4 you and your friends / watch movies / on TV   _____ ? _____ .

4.4 *A/AN*; ADJECTIVES BEFORE NOUNS (page 40)

a/an	adjectives before nouns
Use *a/an* with singular nouns. It means "one." *Do you have **a** laptop? (= 1 laptop)* *This is **an** app for photos. (= 1 app)* Use *a* before consonant sounds (for example, *b, c, d, f,* …): *a tablet, a cookie* Use *an* before vowel sounds (*a, e, i, o, u*): *an app, **an** apartment*	Adjectives go before a noun: *You have a **nice** home.* ✓ *You have a ~~home nice~~.* ✗ *It's an **expensive** laptop. This is a **new** apartment.* *I post **interesting** photos.* The ending of an adjective is the same for singular and plural nouns. Do <u>not</u> add *s* to an adjective. *I like **small** TVs.* ✓ *I like ~~smalls~~ TVs.* ✗

<u>Don't</u> use *a/an* with:	
1 plural nouns: *I like **photos**.*	3 numbers + noun: *I have **one son** and **two daughters**.*
2 *this* + noun: ***This tablet** is nice.*	4 possessive adjectives + noun: ***My phone** is really old.*

A Ⓒircle the correct words to complete the sentences.

1 Do you have *a camera / an camera*?

2 We don't want *a new TV / new a TV*.

3 *Your an apartment / Your apartment* is very nice.

4 I want coffee and *a cookie / a one cookie*.

5 *A game / This game* is really boring.

6 We have *a children / three children*.

7 I don't like *computers / computer*.

8 Do you live in *a apartment / an apartment*?

5.1   SIMPLE PRESENT STATEMENTS WITH *HE, SHE, THEY* (page 45)

Simple present statements with *he, she, they*		
	Affirmative	**Negative**
He / She	**plays** basketball. **goes out** every evening. **watches** TV a lot. **studies** on the weekend. **has** a big house.	**doesn't play** basketball. **doesn't go out** every evening. **doesn't watch** TV a lot. **doesn't study** on weekends. **doesn't have** a big house.
They	**play** soccer. **have** a big house.	**don't play** soccer. **don't have** a big house.

Use *in* to talk about times of day: *I run in the morning.*

Use *on* to talk about days: *I play soccer on Saturdays.*

 Use adverbs of frequency say *how often* you do things.

100%   **always   usually   often   sometimes   hardly ever   never**   0%

Put adverbs of frequency <u>before</u> the verb: *She **sometimes** works on Saturday.*

With pronouns + *be*, adverbs of frequency go <u>after</u> the verb: *I'm **usually** at home in the evening.*

A   **Circle the correct words to complete the sentences.**

1   My sister often *watch / watches* basketball on TV.

2   I don't like coffee, so I *usually / never* drink it.

3   My laptop is old and slow. I *always / hardly ever* use it.

4   My grandma *don't / doesn't* have a cell phone. She *always / hardly ever* calls me from home.

5   My friends are usually at work on Saturday and Sunday. They *have / don't have* free time on the weekend.

5.2   QUESTIONS IN THE SIMPLE PRESENT (page 47)

Simple present: *yes/no* questions			
Yes/no questions			Short answers
Do	I/we	**work** on the weekend?	Yes, I **do** / No, we **don't**.
Do	you	**eat** breakfast?	Yes, I **do**. / No, I **don't**.
Does	she/he	**study** in the evening?	Yes, she **does**. / No, he **doesn't**.
Does	it	**have** two bedrooms?	Yes, it **does**. / No, it **doesn't**.
Do	they	**go** to class on Monday?	Yes, they **do**. / No, they **don't**.

Simple present: information questions				
I / You / We / They	**Where** **What time** **What**	**do** **do** **do**	I / we you they	**go** every day? **get up**? **do** on Saturday?
He / She / It	**Where** **When** **What time**	**does** **does** **does**	he she it	**live**? **meet** her friends? **open**?

What time ... ? and *When ... ?*

A   *What time is it?*
B   *It's 1.30.*
A   *When does he study?*
B   *He studies in the evening.*

A   **Put the words in the correct order to make questions.**

1   lunch? / eat / does / he / Where

2   to / she / go / Does / this school?

3   their / do / meet / friends? / When / they

4   do / work? / you / What / go / to / time

5   soccer / your friends / after work? / play / Do

6.1 THERE'S, THERE ARE; A LOT OF, SOME, NO (page 55)

There's (= there is), there are; a lot, some, no	
Singular (= 1 thing)	**Plural (= 2+ things)**
There's a restaurant near the hotel. = one **There's no** shower in the bathroom. = zero	**There are no** stores on our street. = zero **There are three** bedrooms in the house. = an exact number **There are some** chairs in the kitchen. = a small number **There are a lot of** apps on my phone. = a big number

A **Look at the words in parentheses ( ). Then complete the sentences with the words in the box.**

There's a	There's no	There are no	There are a lot of	There are some

1 _____ parks in the city.   (zero)
2 _____ people in the café.   (a big number)
3 _____ great stores on Pacific Street.   (a small number)
4 _____ park next to the hospital.   (one)
5 _____ restaurant in this museum.   (zero)

6.2 COUNT AND NON-COUNT NOUNS (page 57)

Count nouns (nouns with a singular and plural form)	
Singular Use *There is* with *a* or *an*. There's **a plant**.	**Plural** Use *There are* with *no, some, a lot of*, or a number. There are **no plants**. There are **some plants**. There are **a lot of plants**. There are **two plants**.
Non-count nouns (nouns with no singular or plural form)	
Use *There is* with *no, some,* or *a lot of*. Do <u>not</u> use *a, an*, or a number. There's **no grass**. There's **some grass**. There's **a lot of grass**. ~~There's three grass.~~	

A **Write sentences with *There's* or *There are*. Make some nouns plural.**

1 no / milk / in the refrigerator   *There's no milk in the refrigerator.*
2 a lot of / plant / in my house   _____
3 a / restaurant / in the museum   _____
4 some / sugar / on the table   _____
5 some / small hotel / near here   _____

VOCABULARY PRACTICE

1.1 COUNTRIES AND NATIONALITIES (page 2)

A **Write the country or the nationality.**

1 Are you ___Russian___ ? (Russia)
2 I'm from _____ . (Mexican)
3 I'm _____ . (Ecuador)
4 You're from _____ . (Chilean)

5 Are you _____ ? (Japan)
6 Are you from _____ ? (Brazilian)
7 I'm not _____ . (South Korea)
8 I'm from Madrid. I'm _____ . (Spain)

B <u>Underline</u> **two correct answers for each sentence.**

1 Are you from _Russia_ / Chilean / _South Korea_?
2 I'm from American / _Mexico_ / _Japan_.
3 You're not _French_ / _Peru_ / Colombian.
4 Are you from _New York_ / _Chicago_ / American?

5 I'm not Mexico / _Brazilian_ / _Chinese_.
6 You are _Peruvian_ / _French_ / Chile.
7 Are you _Peruvian_ / Japan / _South Korean_?
8 I'm from Ecuadorian / _Lima_ / _Germany_.

1.2 THE ALPHABET; PERSONAL INFORMATION (page 5)

A **Add <u>five</u> missing letters to the alphabet, in order.**

1 A B C ~~D~~ E F G H I J L M O P Q R T U V W X Z

2 a c d e g h j k l m n o q r s t v w x y z

B **Complete the sentences with the words in the box.**

College	company	email address	first name	last name

1 The name of my _____ is Home Sales, Inc.
2 **A** What's your _____ ? **B** It's jenatkins@abc.net.
3 **A** Hey, Ana. What's your _____ ? **B** It's Gomez. Ana Gomez.
4 I'm a student at Hunter _____ in New York City.
5 **A** Hi, Susie Ball. How do you spell your _____ ? **B** S-U-S-I-E.

2.1 FAMILY; NUMBERS (page 13)

A **Write the words in the chart.**

~~aunt~~	child	daughter	grandfather	husband	parent	son	wife
brother	cousin	father	grandmother	mother	sister	uncle	

Men and women 👫	Women 👩	Men 👨
	aunt	

B Write the numbers.

1 twenty-two _____22_____
2 fifty-one _____
3 thirty-nine _____
4 eighty-three _____

5 forty-six _____
6 sixty-seven _____
7 thirty-eight _____
8 seventy-four _____

9 ninety-five _____
10 twenty-six _____

2.2 DESCRIBING PEOPLE; *REALLY / VERY* (page 14)

A Complete the sentences with the words in the box. You won't use all the words.

friendly	interesting	old	really	short	
shy	smart	boring	tall	young	

1 Carrie is two. She's really _____ .
2 He's a college student. He's _____ .
3 My father is 190 cm. He's very _____ .
4 He's not interesting. He's _____ .
5 My friend Georgio is _____ funny!
6 Ariana is 95. She's very _____ .

B Unscramble the letters in parentheses ( ). Write the adjectives.

1 Susana is _____interesting_____ and really _____ . (nteisreignt) / (tlal)
2 My son is _____ and _____ . (mtras) / (ynufn)
3 My grandfather is _____ and _____ . (dlo) / (rosth)
4 The child is very _____ and _____ . (ynugo) / (ysh)
5 They're _____ and not _____ . (fienrdyl) / (bgrion)

3.1 ROOMS IN A HOME (page 22)

A Read the sentences and complete the words.

1 This is our d_____ a_____ ,
   with a p_____ on the w_____ .
2 This is my sister's b_____ . It's next to the b_____ .
3 This is our dog, Jack. He's on the f_____ .
4 This is the d_____ of our house.
5 This is the l_____ r_____ ,
   with one big w_____ .
6 And this is the k_____ . It's my favorite room.

B Circle the correct word to complete the sentences.

1 My sister is in her *bedroom / floor*.
2 This is the bathroom, with one *wall / window*.
3 This is the *dining area / door* to the kitchen.
4 My family is in the *living room / bathroom* now.
5 The *picture / kitchen* on the wall is interesting.
6 Our cats are on the *door / floor*.

3.2 FURNITURE (page 24)

A **Match the words to the things in the picture.**

chair   ~~couch~~   refrigerator   rug   sink   table   television

1 ___couch___   2 _____   3 _____   4 _____

5 _____   6 _____   7 _____

B (Circle) **the correct words to complete the sentences. Check (✓) the sentences that are true for you.**

1 A big *bed / shower* is in the bedroom. ☐
2 My *rug / bookcase* is really tall. ☐
3 A small *shower / couch* is in the bathroom. ☐
4 My *TV / desk* is really old. It's from the year 1800. ☐
5 I have a small *lamp / chair* on a table in my bedroom. ☐

4.1 TECHNOLOGY (page 34)

A **Complete the sentences with the words in the box. You won't use all the words.**

app   camera   cell phone   earphones   games   laptop   smartwatch   tablet

1 Is that a really big phone, or is it a _____ ?
2 I have a computer. It's a _____ .
3 Yes, I have a _____ . The number is (593) 555-2194.
4 I don't have a _____ , but I have the time on my cell phone.
5 This picture is great! The _____ on your cell phone is really good.
6 My emails are on my phone. I have an email _____ .
7 My computer isn't for work. It's for fun. I have my _____ on it.

B (Circle) **the correct words to complete the sentences.**

1 On my phone, I have a good *laptop / camera*.
2 I have a social media *app / smartwatch* on my tablet.
3 On my laptop, I have a *game / cell phone*.

4.2 USING TECHNOLOGY (page 36)

A **Cross out the word that doesn't belong with each verb.**

1	**call**	friends	social media	family
2	**watch**	movies	videos	text messages
3	**use**	music	technology	apps
4	**post**	cell phone	comments	photos
5	**send**	text messages	email	with friends

B **Complete the sentences with the words in the box.**

chat   listen   play   read   watch

1 I _____ to music with earphones on my tablet.

2 We don't _____ movies on TV.

3 My brother and I _____ games on our tablets.

4 I don't _____ work emails at home.

5 Do you _____ with friends on the internet?

5.1 DAYS AND TIMES OF DAY; EVERYDAY ACTIVITIES (page 44)

A **Read the days and times of day (a–j). Then put them in the correct order (1–10).**

a on Thursday, in the morning ____
b on Tuesday, in the afternoon ____
c on Thursday, in the evening ____
d on Monday, at night   1
e on Sunday, in the morning ____

f on Saturday, in the evening ____
g on Wednesday, in the morning ____
h on Friday, in the afternoon ____
i on Tuesday, in the evening ____
j on Saturday, in the afternoon ____

B **Use phrases from exercise A to complete the sentences so they're true for you. Write an X if you never do the activity.**

1 I go out with friends _____ .

2 I watch TV _____ .

3 I study _____ .

4 I run _____ .

5 I play soccer _____ .

6 I read _____ .

7 I work _____ .

8 I'm in bed _____ .

5.2 TELLING THE TIME (page 46)

A Look at the times (1–8). Then (circle) the correct sentence.

1	3:40	**a** It's twenty to four.		**b** It's forty to three.
2	12:30	**a** It's twenty thirty.		**b** It's twelve thirty.
3	6:15	**a** It's a quarter after six.		**b** It's a quarter to six.
4	12:00 a.m.	**a** It's midnight.		**b** It's noon.
5	1:45	**a** It's a quarter to one.		**b** It's one forty-five.
6	8:07	**a** It's seven to eight.		**b** It's eight-oh-seven.
7	9:15	**a** It's nine fifteen.		**b** It's nine fifty.
8	4:52	**a** It's five forty-two.		**b** It's four fifty-two.

B <u>Underline</u> the correct words to complete the paragraph.

Carmen *gets up* / *goes to* bed at 7:15 a.m. She eats *lunch* / *breakfast* at 7:45. Then she *goes to work* / *gets up*. She usually has *dinner* / *lunch* at 12:30 p.m. She drinks *coffee* / *class* in the afternoon. On Tuesday, she goes to *class* / *lunch* after work – she studies English. She usually eats *dinner* / *coffee* at 7:00. She goes to *bed* / *class* at 11 p.m.

6.1 PLACES IN CITIES (page 54)

A Complete the sentences with the words in the box.

café	college	hotel	museum	park	school	mall	zoo

1 We often eat breakfast in a _____ .

2 I sometimes run in the _____ .

3 The _____ has hundreds of old pictures and a lot of art.

4 The _____ in my neighborhood has 160 children.

5 The students at the _____ are 18 to 22 years old.

6 This is a great _____ . It has a lot of my favorite stores.

7 The rooms in the _____ have bathrooms with showers.

8 The _____ in my city has 20 elephants.

B Cross out <u>one</u> word that does not complete each sentence.

1	We have lunch in a _____ on Saturdays.	*restaurant*	*store*	*park*
2	We learn about things at a _____ .	*school*	*restaurant*	*museum*
3	We shop at the _____ every weekend.	*mall*	*hospital*	*supermarket*
4	The _____ has a big TV.	*park*	*hotel*	*restaurant*
5	She studies English in _____ .	*school*	*college*	*a movie theater*

6.2 NATURE (page 56)

A **Complete the email with the words in the box.**

> flowers   lake   mountain   snow   trees

Reply Forward

Hi Julia,

How are you? I'm great! My new town is *really* cool. I like nature, and there's a lot of nature here! There's a big, tall ¹_____ near my house. There's a forest on the mountain, with a lot of ²_____ . There's ³_____ on top of the mountain in January and February. There's a small ⁴_____ in my neighborhood, and I run next to the water in the morning. There are no ⁵_____ now because it's January.

I love this town. Please visit soon!

Your friend,

Marisa

B **Circle the correct word to complete the sentences.**

1 My house is on the *beach / forest* next to the ocean.

2 There is a lot of *ocean / grass* in the park.

3 There are a lot of plants and flowers in the *forest / lake*.

4 There's a lot of water in the *river / desert*.

5 My grandma and grandpa live near the *ocean / flowers*.

6 A lot of animals eat *plants / mountains*.

7 Donna lives on a small *island / desert* in the Atlantic Ocean.

8 There are a lot of small *grass / hills* here, but there are no mountains.

This page is intentionally left blank

PROGRESS CHECK

Can you do these things? Check (✓) what you can do. Then write your answers in your notebook.

UNIT 1

Now I can …	Prove it
☐ say countries and nationalities.	Write your country and your nationality.
☐ use *I am.*	Write two sentences about you. Use *I'm* and *I'm from.*
☐ use the alphabet to spell words.	Spell your first name and your last name. Spell your email address.
☐ ask and answer questions with *What's … ?* and *It's …* .	Write a question and answer about personal information. Use *What's* and *It's.*
☐ check into a hotel.	Write two questions you hear at a hotel. Write answers to the questions.
☐ write a profile.	Read your profile from lesson 1.4. Find a way to improve it. Use the Accuracy check, Register check, and the new language from this unit.

UNIT 2

Now I can …	Prove it
☐ say family names and numbers.	Write the names and ages of four members of your family. Write the numbers in words.
☐ use *is* and *are.*	Write four sentences with *is* and *are.* Write about you or your family and friends.
☐ use adjectives to describe people.	Complete the sentences with adjectives. *My parents are … My best friend is …*
☐ use *is not* and *are not.*	Make the three sentences negative. *She's tall. We're from Seoul. They're funny.*
☐ talk about ages and birthdays.	When's your birthday? How old is your best friend? Write answers in full sentences.
☐ write a post about friends in a photo.	Read your post about friends from lesson 2.4. Find a way to improve it. Use the Accuracy check, Register check, and the new language from this unit.

UNIT 3

Now I can …	Prove it
☐ talk about rooms in my home.	Write five rooms and five things in rooms.
☐ use possessive adjectives, *'s* and *s'.*	Change the words in parentheses ( ) to possessives. *This is my (brother) bedroom. (He) bedroom is between (I) bedroom and (we) (parents) bedroom.*
☐ talk about furniture.	Write five or more words for furniture.
☐ use *it is.*	Complete the questions. Then answer with your own information. _____ *your home big?* _____ *near your school?*
☐ offer and accept a drink and snack.	Someone says, "Coffee?" Write two different answers.
☐ write an email about a home-share.	Read your email from lesson 3.4. Find a way to improve it. Use the Accuracy check, Register check, and the new language from this unit.

PROGRESS CHECK

Can you do these things? Check (✓) what you can do. Then write your answers in your notebook.

Now I can …

Prove it

☐ talk about my favorite things.

Write about five things you like, love, or want.

☐ use the simple present.

Write about a thing you have and a thing you don't have.

☐ say how you use technology.

Write about three ways you use your phone.

☐ use *yes/no* questions in the simple present.

Complete the questions. Then write the answers with your own information. _____ *you use apps on your phone?*
_____ *you and your parents chat online?*

☐ ask questions to develop a conversation.

Complete the conversation.
A _____ *social media?*
B Yes, I do. _____ ?

☐ write product reviews.

Read your product reviews from lesson 4.4. Find a way to improve them. Use the Accuracy check, Register check, and the new language from this unit.

Now I can …

Prove it

☐ use days and times of days with everyday activities.

Write two things you do on weekdays in the morning. Write two things you do on Saturday.

☐ use the simple present and adverbs of frequency.

Complete the sentences. Write about your friends.
_____ *always* _____ *on the weekend.*
_____ *and* _____ *never* _____
in the evening.

☐ tell the time and talk about routines.

What time is it now? When do you get up on weekdays? What time do you usually have dinner? Write answers in full sentences.

☐ ask *yes/no* and information questions in the simple present.

Complete the questions with *do* or *does*. Then write your answers.
What time _____ *you get up on Saturday? Where*
_____ *you and your friends eat lunch on Monday?*
_____ *your teacher have lunch at school?*

☐ show you agree or have things in common.

Read the statements. Write responses that are true for you.
Soccer is fun.   I never run.

☐ write a report.

Read your WRAP report from lesson 5.4. Find a way to improve it. Use the Accuracy check, Register check, and the new language from this unit.

Now I can …

Prove it

☐ use words for places in a city.

Write about six places in a city.

☐ use *there's / there are* with *a/an, some, a lot of, no.*

Write four true sentences for your city. Use the sentences below.
There are _____ *in my city. / There's* _____
in my neighborhood.

☐ use words for places in nature.

Write about six places in nature.

☐ use count and non-count nouns.

Write about the plants, trees, and grass in your neighborhood.

☐ ask for and give simple directions.

Write one way to ask for directions and one way to give directions.

☐ write a fact sheet.

Read your fact sheet from lesson 6.4. Find a way to improve it. Use the Accuracy check, Register check, and the new language from this unit.

PAIR WORK PRACTICE (STUDENT A)

1.3 EXERCISE 5C   STUDENT A

1 You are Sandra, the visitor. Give your information to your partner.

2 You are the hotel clerk. Ask for your partner's information. Complete the hotel card.

HOTEL INFORMATION CARD:
City Bed & Breakfast

First name:	Sandra
Last name:	Mills
Number of nights:	Three
Email:	sandra85@listmail.net
Phone number:	367 555 0219
Company/School:	Big City Travel

HOTEL INFORMATION CARD:
Tree House Hotel

First name:	
Last name:	
Number of nights:	
Email:	
Phone number:	
Company/School:	

2.3 EXERCISE 3D   STUDENT A

1 Say a person from the table. Say the incorrect birthday. Then correct yourself.

> Anna. Her birthday is August 15. No, sorry, August <u>13</u>.

Person	Anna	Martin	Paulo	Rosa	Jacob
Incorrect birthday	August 15	December 2	June 5	October 21	April 12
Correct birthday	August <u>13</u>	December <u>3</u>	<u>July</u> 5	October <u>31</u>	April <u>20</u>

2 Listen to your partner. Write the correct birthday. Circle the correction (the number or the month).

Person	Gloria	Larry	Helena	Susan	Bruno
Incorrect birthday	September 13	November 6	May 9	February 30	January 25
Correct birthday					

4.3 EXERCISE 2D   STUDENT A

1 Follow the flow chart. Use the topics in the box or your own ideas. Talk about two or three topics.

laptops	music videos
social media	video chat

2 Follow the flow chart. Talk about the topics your partner chooses.

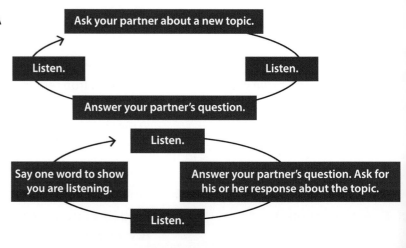

5.3 EXERCISE 2D   STUDENT A

1   **Choose <u>one</u> of the jobs in the box. <u>Don't</u> tell your partner. Then complete the sentences about the job with** *always, usually, often, sometimes, hardly ever,* **or** *never.*

doctor   hotel clerk   server   student

1 I _____ get up early.   4 I _____ work with friends.   7 I _____ go to bed late.

2 I _____ eat at home.   5 I _____ read books.   8 I _____ work on the

3 I _____ have free time.   6 I _____ send emails for work.   weekend.

2   **Your partner is a teacher, salesperson, chef, or artist. Ask questions and guess the job.**

> Do you get up early?   Always.   Do you eat at home?   Never.   Are you a … ?

3   **Your partner asks you questions. Answer with <u>one or two</u> words. Your partner guesses your job.**

6.3 EXERCISE 2D   STUDENT A

Give the directions below to Student B. Student B repeats and you listen. Is it correct?

1   Turn left here. Then go straight. It's on the left.

2   It's over there. Go two blocks. Turn right. Then turn right again.

3   Turn left here. Then turn left again. It's on the right.

PAIR WORK PRACTICE (STUDENT B)

1.3 EXERCISE 5C   STUDENT B

1   You are the hotel clerk. Ask for your partner's information. Complete the hotel card.

2   You are Tom, the visitor. Give your information to your partner.

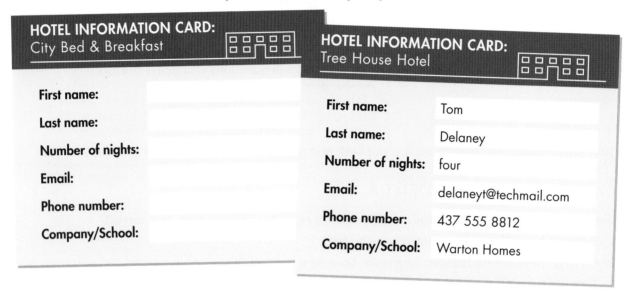

HOTEL INFORMATION CARD:
City Bed & Breakfast

First name:

Last name:

Number of nights:

Email:

Phone number:

Company/School:

HOTEL INFORMATION CARD:
Tree House Hotel

First name: Tom

Last name: Delaney

Number of nights: four

Email: delaneyt@techmail.com

Phone number: 437 555 8812

Company/School: Warton Homes

2.3 EXERCISE 3D   STUDENT B

1   Listen to your partner say the incorrect birthdays, and then the correct birthdays. Write the correct birthday. <u>Underline</u> the correction (the number or the month).

Person	Anna	Martin	Paulo	Rosa	Jacob
Incorrect birthday	August 15	December 2	June 5	October 21	April 12
Correct birthday					

2   Say a person from the table. Say the incorrect birthday. Then correct yourself.

> Gloria. Her birthday is September 13. No, sorry, September 30.

Person	Gloria	Larry	Helena	Susan	Bruno
Incorrect birthday	September 13	November 6	May 9	February 30	January 25
Correct birthday	September **30**	November **16**	**March** 9	February **20**	January 2**4**

4.3 EXERCISE 2D   STUDENT B

1 Follow the flow chart. Talk about the topics your partner chooses.

2 Follow the flow chart. Use the topics in the box or your own ideas. Talk about two or three topics.

laptops	music videos
social media	video chat

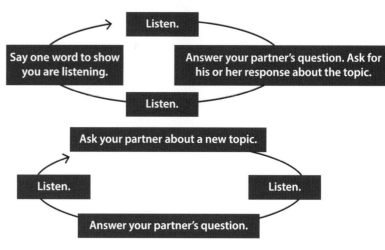

5.3 EXERCISE 2D   STUDENT B

1 Choose <u>one</u> of the jobs in the box. <u>Don't</u> tell your partner. Then complete the sentences about the job with *always, usually, often, sometimes, hardly ever,* or *never.*

artist	chef	salesperson	teacher

1 I _____ get up early.   4 I _____ work with friends.   7 I _____ go to bed late.

2 I _____ eat at home.   5 I _____ read books.   8 I _____ work on the weekend.

3 I _____ have free time.   6 I _____ send emails for work.

2 Your partner asks you questions. Answer with <u>one or two</u> words. Your partner guesses your job.

3 Your partner is a student, doctor, server, or hotel clerk. Ask questions and guess the job.

6.3 EXERCISE 2D   STUDENT B

Give the directions below to Student A. Student A repeats and you listen. Is it correct?

1 Turn left. Go straight. That's San Gabriel Street.

2 Go straight. Then turn right. It's on the right.

3 Turn right here. Turn right again. Then turn left. It's on the right.

This page is intentionally left blank

This page is intentionally left blank

This page is intentionally left blank

This page is intentionally left blank

This page is intentionally left blank

This page is intentionally left blank

This page is intentionally left blank